LE CHIC COCOON

7 Steps to Creating Your Selfish Space

JENNIFER DUCHENE

Dearest Lisa,
Soul Sister, Much Love
Friend, & Laughter!
Big Light
en Duchene

ENDORSEMENTS

Empowering, enlightening and thoroughly enjoyable reading! Jennifer's bold and spot-on assessment of a woman's entitlement to her very own 'patch of peace' is both liberating and refreshing.

Baring her own soul and sharing her personal experiences adds an intimacy that readers will identify with and reinforces the common bond that we women share. The simple-to-follow action steps enable any woman, regardless of space or resources, to create and start reveling in her very own Chic Cocoon.

SANDY DIXON
THE STAGING TRAINER
WWW.THESTAGINGTRAINER.COM

In today's busy world more is expected of us than ever. As women, not only we must manage family, household and career, but we must do so meet the high expectations set by society. Our fast-paced lives offer us little opportunity to slow down, never mind time to nurture ourselves. For those of us with young children finding a "Room of One's Own" is not only difficult but nearly impossible, yet it is crucial to our well-being. Go ahead, celebrate, do something nice for yourself - pick up your copy of Le Chic Cocoon today. This makes a delightful pairing with your favorite bottle of bubbly!

JESSICA GORDON RYAN
MEMOIRIST, SOCIAL MEDIA EXPERT, WRITER, EDITORIAL AND CREATIVE
DIRECTOR OF LIFESTYLE BLOGS... BY DAY - CHAMPAGNE AND GIMLET
DRINKER BY NIGHT!

Every woman needs a space to call her own that reflects who she truly is. Le Chic Cocoon is a practical step-by-step guide to creating that essential space for yourself.

JUDY PEEBLES, THE JOURNALING JENIUS™
AND CREATOR OF THE KNOWLEDGE SERIES – YOUR KEY TO SUCCESS

Le Chic Cocoon an insightful blend of personal storytelling and artful brilliance from a talented designer. Jen Duchene takes a creative and courageous stand while showing you how to translate the language of your soul into a nourishing environment that reflects the rich, unique, expressive woman you truly are.

TAMBRA HARCK
SPIRITUAL MENTOR, AUTHOR, SPEAKER
WEB: TAMBRAHARCK.COM
BOOK: SACREDTRUTHSBOOK.COM

You deserve your own Chic Cocoon, and with lots of sass, spunk, wit and humor, Jennifer makes it safe to discover your fabulous inner core and selfish, sacred space! Jen is a key, unlocking the door to the strength and beauty inside you, welcoming you to a room of your own, and showing you how to deck out your delicious surroundings and feed your soul.

KELLY GALEA
AUTHOR, SPEAKER, COACH PROVIDING INSPIRATION AND SOLUTIONS
FOR CREATIVE ENTREPRENEURS AT DESIGNBIZCOACH.COM AND
FROMCORPORATETOCREATIVE.COM

I've never run across a book that made me realize just how important I am in this world and that I really do need to put myself first. I'm recommending this book to every client, friend, and women in my life.

ALARA K. CASTELL
YOUR SASSY SPIRITUAL GUIDE

Duchene is masterful at keeping her finger on the pulse of the female psyche through Le Chic Cocoon. While her inspiration comes from Virginal Woolf, Duchene is able to bring the concept of "a room of one's own" to the modern "super woman." Through her 7 steps, Duchene walks us through the why as well as the how to create our Cocoons. Personally: On my 39th birthday, I decided to be "selfish." I said no to friends and family who wanted to move in and claimed the guest room as my photography studio. I put my mental, emotional, physical and spiritual health before anyone else's. I carved out time for myself. I started to decorate my office, not just work in it with my eyes only pointed to my computer screen. Jen's book gave me so many more ideas of how to make those rooms truly a reflection of ME. I am inspired.

JILLIAN TODD
JILLIAN TODD PORTRAIT COUTURE

In Jen Duchene's Le Chic Cocoon you get the whole metamorphosis: witty, wise expertise for creating "a room of your own," and even deeper support for filling it with your most treasured possession: the unvarnished truth of yourself."

MARIDEL BOWES
"SHAKING UP A COCKTAIL OF SPIRIT AND SOUL WITH A TWIST OF
LAUGHTER" WWW.EVOLVINGJOURNEY.COM

Emotional, supportive, spiritual! Jennifer Duchene effectively combines design elements into the integral woman, reaching deep into the core of who she is and what she's all about. It's all about living your dreams…in bright and beautiful color.

PATTI MCKENNA
COPYWRITER, EDITOR, AND AUTHOR OF *CHILDREN SHOULD COME
WITH WARNING LABELS* AND *FROM A LULLABY TO GOODBYE*

LE CHIC COCOON
7 Steps to Creating Your Selfish Space

Jennifer Duchene

Copyright© 2011
ISBN 978-1-937445-07-2
Library of Congress Control Number: 2011936502

Published by Bush Street Press
237 Kearny Street, #174
San Francisco, CA 94108
415-413-0785

The information provided in this book is designed to provide helpful information about the subjects discussed. This book is not meant to be used, nor should it be used, to diagnose or treat any medical condition. For diagnosis or treatment of any medical problem, consult your own physician. The author and publisher disclaim all liability associated with the recommendations and guidelines set forth in this book. References are provided for informational purposes only and do not constitute endorsement of any websites or other sources. Readers should be aware that the websites listed in this book may change.

This is a self-help book that covers my philosophy, thoughts, and opinion relating to creating a space of your own. While I have used personal anecdotes, written to the best of my recollection, my family or anyone mentioned in this book are not responsible for anything I experienced. I take full responsibility for my own life. Names and identities of people in my stories have been changed to protect their privacy. Some people have agreed to be quoted, and I have included their names. Any errors made are my own.

Moving furniture can be harmful to your body, so make sure you use equipment and tools, like furniture slides, take precautions, and get help if you need it. If you choose to move furniture, you do so at your own risk.

This is not an anti-men book. I love men, and I think they are an essential part of life on earth. Procreation, relationships, and children are a delicious and necessary element. This book was written for women, no matter their sexual orientation, because I know personally, from my own journey, how we as women need a place to call our own. I am stating myths that I have seen. That does not mean I agree with any of the myths or that I personally experienced every one of them. We are all different and valuable, no matter our sex.

DEDICATION

I dedicate this book to Leslie Carothers for believing in me.

TABLE OF CONTENTS

I have always been a "selfish woman." At an early age, I saw the value of taking care of myself in order to be better for others. Maybe it was through watching my mom, who never really had a sense of the beautiful butterfly she really was. Having a selfish space and time for her "self" in her home was set aside. Instead, she was locked in the bedroom that she shared with her abuser. To this day, I still don't think she has been able to claim her space (step 3 in this book) as her own. Out of college, I started my career, counseling abused and neglected teenage girls, and I learned about the importance of my own Cocoon. My home was always a Cocoon of sorts. It was a place to tuck away and "Be Selfish." And as my career evolved and I worked with more and more women under stress, loss, frustration, and loneliness, that space was very important.

But I had a myth (step one in this book, Uncover Your Myths) that kept my Cocoon from allowing me to fully find my nirvana (step 7 of Jen's book) and transformative process. My myth for my own room started with "real life." Not one, but two, house fires, the destruction of space, of things with meaning, all gone, led me to believe that "space" really did not matter, that things were not that important. So decorating a Cocoon and truly claiming my space was not important for many years of my adult life.

When I found my true Le Chic Cocoon, I had to create awareness of this myth and change it forever. Getting in touch with the true spirit of "who" I am and why that matters in the physical space around me allowed me to create a space that was 100% all mine. My Le Chic Cocoon is now my office. It is a glorious space full of light and natural wood and inspirational quotes and color. (Feisty Red is the primary wall color, if you were wondering!) This room has changed my life and business tremendously! It welcomes me every morning. It encourages my creativity. It nurtures the speaker and coach in me. And selfishly, it is all mine.

So many women take their space and its purpose for granted. I live with intention in my entire home now. I have taken each room and thought about the parts of me that need to be nurtured in that space. I have done little things that allow me to walk into that space and be reminded of its intention. That is what this book can become for you.

I have known Jen for years and have watched her blossom into the most delightful butterfly. Her own self-discovery about creating and having sacred space is a special one. She thoughtfully and lovingly sacrificed "selfish" for her daughter, living in a relationship which did not truly fulfill her heart and soul. As I am sure many of you can relate, Jen has no regrets, but until that chapter ended in her life, she did not realize how much she needed to take care of herself, to nurture self, to create her own nirvana of happiness. Through her own self-discovery, she taught me to stop listening to everyone else and embrace the colors of who I am. *Le Chic Cocoon* will lead you through the seven steps she discovered along her own path.

What's even more exciting is that Jennifer will show you that you have everything you need, physically, mentally, and emotionally, to create your Le Chic Cocoon. As a designer, she knows that often the things that make us feel most special are already in our home—we just need the steps to create it.

Since 1997, I have traveled the world, speaking to audiences of women about stress, owning their lives, being empowered and happy. I recall teaching a seminar in Bath England. A woman came to me at the break wanting to speak privately, tears in her eyes. She shared with me a story of how lost she is, pulled in every direction in her life. Her manager, her husband, her mother, her children all seemed to take priority in her life. She wanted to take care of herself first for a change and wanted a resource to take with her, something that could help her learn to care for who she is. As I turned the pages of this book, I so vividly remembered this woman and I wished it was the one I had to give her.

Today, I meet women just like her. They are beautiful, amazing women, with no place to call their own. This book is for you and for them. If you are a woman like me who has always created space for yourself, this book is still for you. Each will discover a path to creating a space on a deeper level of self-love and nurturing.

Jen's book will give you the opportunity to discover everything that is in YOU through creating your own Le Chic Cocoon. Through the evolution of seven steps, she will walk you through your own transformation. There is power in having an external space that creates intention and cares for the deepest part of who you are. As Jen says, "Be Selfish." I believe every woman should. Greater self-love and nurturing leads to greater other love and happiness, and you deserve it. I personally love learning from someone who not only has the expertise professionally, but the personal story I can relate to; Jennifer does both with beautiful words and a spirit of love.

You deserve nirvana and happiness. Nestle in with this book. Take the time to explore each step on a personal level. Build your Le Chic Cocoon and let the world bask in your happiness.

Ann Evanston

Ann M. Evanston, MA, is a motivational speaker, coach, and consultant whose passion and purpose is inspiring others to discover their REAL edge. She can easily be found online and would love you to say hi. annevanston.com

AUTHOR'S NOTE

Who is the real Virginia Woolf?

Woolf had an enormous effect on me as a young woman. She was a phenomenal writer who still influences thought, literature, and society, 70 years after her death. Her famous line, "A woman must have money and a room of her own if she is to write fiction," is why I chose Woolf's quotes to begin every chapter in this book. You may not be writing fiction, but even today, I believe a woman needs a room of her own to create her own inspired life.

> Adeline Virginia Woolf (pronounced /ˈwʊlf/; 25 January 1882 – 28 March 1941) was an English author, essayist, publisher, and writer of short stories, regarded as one of the foremost modernist literary figures of the twentieth century.
>
> During the interwar period, Woolf was a significant figure in London literary society and a member of the Bloomsbury Group. Her most famous works include the novels *Mrs. Dalloway* (1925), *To the Lighthouse* (1927) and *Orlando* (1928), and the book-length essay *A Room of One's Own* (1929)
>
> *from Wikipedia
> http://en.wikipedia.org/wiki/Virginia_Woolf

INTRODUCTION

"LOCK UP YOUR LIBRARIES IF YOU LIKE, BUT THERE IS NO GATE, NO LOCK, NO BOLT THAT YOU CAN SET UPON THE FREEDOM OF MY MIND."

--Virginia Woolf (*A Room of One's Own*)

What pulled me into creating the idea of a Chic Cocoon was the frisson of discovery, while driving home one day, of how little women's lives have changed since Virginia Woolf wrote *A Room of One's Own.*

Certainly, how little my life had changed. Freedom may have beckoned over and over, but I had been too afraid to heed the call. My ex-husband was off seeking romance, and the divorce papers were final. I was on a new journey.

What would it take to make me plunge into living and write my own rules?

Picture it, a middle-aged woman hot in the pursuit of another weekend of self-discovery. Only this time, my intuition was leading, not my head. Ready to risk it all, I was transfixed by the incredible conversation I was having with someone who was not visible in my car!

While my nurturing heart was filled with the need to inspire, feed, and fill others and foster connectivity first, I was forgetting to remember me. Overwhelmed, I was still apologizing, always taking second place, and yet filled with discontent.

I realized how much women struggle to find their place, precisely because we are looking at our lives through the eyes of others, failing to loosen apron strings to myth and obligation.

I have walked my own journey, as a woman who has accepted life blindfolded, without stepping back to connect to my heart, not taking a moment out of time to feel if this is was what I wanted.

Discovering on that day that I could mesh my expertise—design with my mission—first you need a room of your own—was passion juice for my soul. A book was born, but first there was a room.

Chic Cocoon

There has been an upswing in men spaces, commonly known as man caves—a room where a guy can relax in his recliner, watch ESPN, hang out with his buddies or play foosball. I can certainly understand why. We all need a place we can escape to that feels safe and familiar. I am smiling as I write this because it makes me think of when we were teenagers. Guys typically recreated that dark basement hangout, and us women were drawn to what captured us as girls becoming women—a boudoir to pamper ourselves in, with face masks, manicures, writing dear diary, and trying on clothes and shoes!

He gets his cave, and you get your own turret to relax, create, and rejuvenate. Finally, you have a place where you can recapture an essence of who you are, before you became a wife, a mom, an employee.

Chic Cocoon is a space for a woman to escape into, both real and imaginary. A woman's retreat, it's a place to explore and nourish her core self. It is a room of one's own to delight in, to create in, to become whole in. Outside rules have no place in your room.

When the door is barred to external tasks, you can dream your impossible dreams. That's Chic Cocoon.

Why Chic Cocoon and not woman cave, diva den, or cozy nest? I chose Chic Cocoon because it feels soft, safe, and secret—a place where a woman can evolve from caterpillar to butterfly. I wanted a new concept, with no preconceived ideas about the woman inside. Some women don't think of themselves as a diva or a cave dweller. And that is okay. Chic Cocoon is the space you invent. It's that getaway room that gives you permission to be you—no matter who she is.

When we can touch the depth of who we are, we open up our wings.

The Divine Feminine is about drawing yourself to your sacred space, tapping into your buried powers. Many times we hide the truth about ourselves or our abilities beneath layers of memory and stories—stories we tell ourselves or that other people told us.

Well, let's change that story. Let's claim our true selves.

THE MOST COURAGEOUS ACT IS STILL
TO THINK FOR YOURSELF.
ALOUD.

--*Coco Chanel*

CHAPTER ONE

Myth to Mastery

"THE EYES OF OTHERS OUR PRISONS;
THEIR THOUGHTS OUR CAGES."
— *Virginia Woolf*

What a powerful truth. How many of us women have lived our lives by the words of Virginia Woolf, without a moment's thought? Eyes locked in tunnel vision. Looking straight ahead. Creeping along the ground. Marching in tune with all the other caterpillars. Allowing others to determine what we see, what we believe. Imprisoning us as surely as if we were in a cage.

Life is full of epiphanies, mythical answers to world problems, and then suddenly you look up and discover that the dishes are still waiting to be washed and the dust bunnies are dancing. For a moment, the world turned and the tasks remained.

I am a designer and a professional decorator. I choose to work with what people already have in their homes, because I believe that we have an emotional connection to our possessions. There is a history and a patina that curates the backdrop of our lives.

I lead people through the process, as opposed to dictating what they should do. I guess you could call it Design Intervention. I honor their homes, their collections, and their lifestyles, and I make their rooms sing. What use is a room if you don't feel good when you are inside?

Naturally, I was happy working this way for many years, building up my practice, and working at honing my entrepreneurial skills. I had created sanctuaries for my clients, but never for myself. I understood their needs, but I never stopped to understand mine. I made my home attractive, warm, and welcoming, but I built in no personal retreat, very little me time. I didn't think I deserved to come first, ever. Then I experienced a personal crisis. My life veered off the safe course I had envisioned. Teetering on the wall of divorce, my life was spiraling out of control. Who was I? How was I going to exist? I had to dig deep into a well of my own truth and build myself up again. Ponder how I had traveled so far from who I thought I was. Other people's thoughts did not make me. That moment of self-discovery created a need for a Chic Cocoon of my own. Embroiled in the fabric of my own story, I could not move without letting go of myths I had swallowed for half a century. I realized that day that this was a universal truth for many women, and Virginia Woolf came to mind.

My search has brought me a new understanding, a greater passion. I am combining my design expertise with my desire to help other women create their own personal spaces. I am committed to helping other women discover self-knowledge, before they implode like I did, not knowing who I was, stripped of my roles.

As women, we typically have nowhere to go where we can just be. Every room in the home has a task demanding to be done. My plan is to give you the impetus to create your retreat from it all, your Chic Cocoon.

An artist, extremely shy and lacking in self-confidence when growing up, I did not know how to connect to my voice.

It has taken me 50 years to understand how important self-love, putting herself first, and owning up to her talents are for a woman.

Some women slip into a dream world, and some women become warriors. Many women have embraced independence. They are strong, vibrant, driven women, who have their own myths to unravel and demystify. Many women are seen as a liability in the corporate world because they can bear children. Sometimes women get wrapped up in the fear of what will happen to their career and life if they have children, before there is even a glimmer of child. I have heard women talk about the fact that we still have not broken the pattern and kicked in the door. I believe what is stopping us is our willingness to believe the myths, precisely because we have not claimed our power. Our strength comes from within. We cannot find it outside ourselves. We must bar the door and lock it, and while away sunny hours behind closed doors in a room of our own so that we can garner the strength that comes from introspection and selfish activity. When we know who we are, we will not care what other people think. We will make choices based on our own rules and needs.

We need to soar in Spirit and connect with our Inner Goddess. We need to trample the myths that impede our progress.

Basically, I bought into the myth as a young girl, believing that considering my own needs was a sin that needed stamping out. So I stamped as hard as I could. My life lessons are twofold—guilt and shame—apparently, this is a common life lesson. Oh, how I struggled to keep my head up high while drowning in my own spit. Guilty for not considering others, for being unkind, I felt shame for not living up to what I perceived to be real. I played the role of the polite woman to the hilt, the try-to-be-pretty-and-pleasing woman. Burying anger, hurt, and disappointment, I swallowed my own poison along with other people's half-baked truths and opinions. If my diva hates housework, so be it. My life is on my terms; **I deserve to be selfish**. So do you.

You deserve to follow your inner Cocoonista.

"Of all the things I lost, I miss my mind the most" is a quote on a postcard on my refrigerator, reminding me that sometimes we do need to lose our minds to find ourselves. It is in the grief that occurs when we can go no lower than a caterpillar that transforms us. But why wait for grief?

The Tale of Many Myths

Perhaps you were fed the dream as a little girl. Barbie is hot, sexy, capable, and even brilliant, and she is desperate for Ken to make her whole. Cinderella has a fairy godmother; she is stunning and has skills like no one's business. Her stepmother is a bitch, and Cinders just takes it, because she is a true a princess. So she hangs out at the fireplace in rags, sweeping and sighing till a prince discovers the shoe fits and carries her off to a castle to live happily ever after. No one knows what indignities she suffers as woman who couldn't say no. This is all part of the myths that we swallow when we allow other people's assumptions and opinions to rule our actions, when we are shamed into giving up what we truly long for.

Saying nothing, but bearing resentment and keeping score, is a tale of many women who were raised to hide their true selves from the world. This brings to mind a harem. Creating an outer shell that covers the inner desires so well creates real walls, roles or not. For most women, the knowledge of what they want or who they are is hidden behind a veil of myth.

What convenient barriers have you hidden behind? I used to believe that settling for what others wanted was good enough for me.

The fear of not being liked was my own secret shame that I crumbled beneath. I was always trying to smooth the waters, making nice, so I could be part of the in crowd. Every time a myth crumbles, my strength grows.

What about you? What myths are you holding sacred? Are you willing to wear body armor and fight the bloody battle? Topple myths? Garner points. Win yourself back?

Subterfuge has always been given a seat at the table.

Girls were raised to pretend. I think many still are, in spite of being encouraged to reach for their dreams. Women are expected to fulfill the traditional roles of housewife, mother and to earn a living. Many strive to be independent and consider being "only a housewife" as a position of shame. Another myth.

At one time, women could not wait to get out of the kitchen and into the boardroom. Now, many relinquish the boardroom to raise their children. A career woman is often exhausted from constantly changing hats. The role of harried housewife, because someone must be there for the children, is no easy task. Often out of guilt or myth, women bear the biggest burden of running the household, no matter what else they do, in spite of the fact that partners are doing more at home.

The myth that won't die, a woman puts her needs last.

I believe being a true housewife is a job that requires incredible skill. Any woman who takes on that role with gusto is not only smart, she is dismissing a myth that no longer matters.

Sometimes when a woman is perceived as being "too much like a man*," those of her own gender fall upon her like turkeys do when one of their ilk starts to bleed†. Why do some women join the conspiracy to belittle their own? I think it's because it is part of a myth they have learned and habitually keep alive. Happily, I have witnessed a growing force of resilient, supportive women who are leading through compassion and sharing.

We need to embrace both our masculine and feminine sides to create balance in our lives.

Women are often cut low, through a knee jerk reaction. Every time someone kicks you down, it is because they are afraid—afraid that you will succeed, make them look bad, or

---

* Turkeys do attack one another—I have seen it.
† Another myth that tough women are not feminine.

because they think you need saving. Their perceptions, too, are driven by myth.

Subterfuge has always been given a seat at the table.

Short leashes, and very little money; that is how we come full circle. When woman have no money and scant knowledge of the world of money, then owning power is impossible, for money is the currency of our world. Women are paid less, in all sorts of ways. Fewer dollars mean less respect, less time, less freedom. Money talks. The fear of not having money keeps us chained to myth and jailer.

When we take charge, we make things happen. We stop being doormats.

We become Keys.

Take the key and unlock the door. It all begins with a room. Every day is a new lesson. A new layer of onion falls transparent and forgotten to the floor. Let go of Myth and create your own reality, no matter what that is.

It took the longest time for me to wake up and realize that my life and my surroundings are in the palm of my hands. Create the life and the space you want right now. Don't wait for someday, or someone, to right your world. Perfection doesn't exist, nor do fairytale princesses, that's just another myth in the coffin. I am surrounded by fabulous, encouraging, inspiring women who help me daily, and I am in gratitude. Embrace women as your sisters. Celebrate with them.

NEITHER MYTH NOR MORTAL CAN TOUCH OUR POWER UNLESS WE ALLOW IT.

OUR LIVES LOOK EXACTLY HOW WE SHAPE THEM IN WORD AND DEED.

I asked some powerful women I know to share a myth, and this is what Alara Castell explained:

One of the myths I had about being a woman was that it was not okay to be sexy. If I was to be sexy, then I would attract all the wrong men and I would give the wrong impression. This hindered the way that I would dress and the way that I would BE in this world.

It wasn't until I was about to get married that I realized something was missing and I was totally disconnected from my body. I wanted to feel sexy! I wanted to feel like a woman! I yearned to be fully connected to all of me.

I listened to my body to see what it desired most and it desired to move sensually, to feel the curves of my body, to love myself whole, to release and to be in an orgasmic state of mind. It's like this saying I heard from a movie once, "Dance is the therapy for the body and soul."

Today, I make sure that I have a space that I love, that totally brings me pleasure with all the yummy goodness I love. In this space, I move every day to get connected to my sensual goddess within.

One of my favorite things to do is to wake up early in the morning, when it's still dark outside, when you can hear the silence of people still sleeping peacefully in their beds, and to stand there naked in front of the mirror and move sensually and repeat, "I love myself, I'm amazing, I'm beautiful, I am enough just as I am."

I make sure to move my hips, to caress my body, to move my hands through my hair, to embrace and love all of me. It's so important to love you and to not lose that love. I love bringing movement into my workshops and into the work I do with women because it's one thing that is lacking in many women's lives, and I believe it's a MUST HAVE.

Alara K. Castell
Your Sassy Spiritual Guide
www.alaracastell.com

We don't have to accept less than we want.

We don't have to compromise with what we want. We get to choose what sacrifices are worth it for us. It is our life, our choices and, yes, our attitude that fashions exactly who we are.

You have gifts you come bearing. You don't need a wise man to bestow anything on you. You need only inner strength, love of yourself, painstakingly built by habit. Can you look into the mirror and declare your love for you as is, less than perfect but perfectly wonderful, nonetheless? If you are willing to be uncomfortable, you can win this awkward battle. When I first read Louise Hay's book, *You Can Heal Your Life*, I could barely look myself in the eye. Now I can do it, easily. Try it. Habit is a wonderful thing. We got ourselves into this mess through habit—the habit of believing other peoples' truths. Why not kick the bad habits to the curb and replace them with good habits?

If each of us had to replace ONE habit that stifles us with one that frees us, we could shape our world. Now that is real power!

Nobody objects to a woman being a good writer or sculptor or geneticist if at the same time, she manages to be a good wife, a good mother, good-looking, good-tempered, well-dressed, well-groomed, and unaggressive.

--MARY MANNES

My Passion for Decorating

I want to teach women, every woman, to embrace her Selfish Space.

I am passionate about helping you to create the space you deserve, right now, using what you have in your home to live in an environment that pleases.

Women need to own the way they live.

No Excuses Living

Stop waiting in line for someday. Shake up your room; let your retreat reflect you.

Every woman deserves to live laughing, to embrace her lifestyle.

A well-decorated home should be a staple of everyday life. No one should have to wait for someday to live in an oasis. I want to give you the tools to create rooms that speak to your heart and your head. I am the Home Makeover Mixtress, blending lifestyle, laughter, and Chic Cocoons. Society may have taught that designers and decorators are for the wealthy, that they are snobs who want you to buy lots of expensive furniture and fill your home with grand pieces that have no personal meaning. This is a myth. I personally know many talented dedicated and un-snobby designers. They are dedicated and as passionate as I about what they do. Some, indeed, may serve the wealthy, and that is their choice.

As a woman who attended design school, studied and mastered various modalities, including redesign, color, trends, and history, soaking it all up like a sponge, I cannot fathom a life that does not incorporate beauty that is comfortable. That is real. I prescribe to William Morris's theory that one should have only what is both beautiful and functional in a home. Discovering redesign was a boon. I love the challenge of taking what is there, no matter how humble, and creating beauty for the owner. One of my clients who had very little to work with, and most of it from consignment stores, told me I have the ability to make junk shine. To me, that is the ultimate compliment. I know a dirty little secret: It is not what you have, but where it is placed that can turn a jumble of mismatched items into your personal palace. People say home is where the heart is. I believe everyone creates their home with pieces of their heart. We may buy with our pocketbooks, but we dream with our heart. We collect treasures along the way that speak to us, like photos and mementos that reflect our history and our journey. This is where our story lies. That is why for so many of us, it is difficult to let go of our belongings. You can let go, once you understand that the tapestry that is woven in a room is not all you are. It is a snapshot. My gift is that I help my clients create a space for transforming their daily lives, moving furniture and accessories around the room, bringing in color, and guiding my clients to thoughtful purchases that complete their spaces in their own voices. The re-arranged rooms honor and cherish the occupants. Best of all, they bestow confidence to live and laugh in.

The Myth Monkeys

It's like the story of the monkeys.

Harry Frederick Harlow http://clearwater-uk.com/MyBlog/2010/02/28/five-monkeys-a-banana-and-corporate-culture/ did this experiment years ago, where they put a bunch of monkeys in a cage who were hungry. There was a banana on the top of a ladder, which they had to climb up to reach. So naturally, the monkeys started climbing, and as they did, they were sprayed with ice water. The monkeys were so shocked they ran down the ladder and would not climb up again, even though they were hungry. A new monkey was added to the cage, and he wanted to climb for the banana, but the myth monkeys on the ground beat up the new monkey, so he was too afraid to climb up. Eventually, there were monkeys who had never ever been up the ladder, because every other monkey had stopped them with force. As human beings, we tend to follow the leaders, believe what other people force upon us about how we should behave and what we should think. We rarely just go for it. We hover over our crowd fear–trapped and self righteous–as if all our "good behavior" is going to save us. Nothing can save us from starving if we don't grab the banana that is waiting.

A woman needs a room to reflect in, a space to awaken her sleeping goddess, locked away from prying eyes and critical voices.

To break the mould of occupying overwhelm, awash in a life overflowing with benign tasks, without a lifeboat in sight, grab your lifeboat and get in. Whether you have a real room or a getaway walk, whether you want to write an opus or watch reruns, mark your territory and your habit.

Create an invisible or visible wall around that space, around the time you claim.

Make your time and needs your number one priority. Rejuvenate. Vibrate. Separate from everything else except She.

Myth Mastery

There are as many myths as there are women. Most of them are designed to dilute our power. There are women who love being in the kitchen, who love taking care of kids, and who are superb housekeepers. I am not knocking them. I applaud their talents. A whole woman is the sum of many parts, just like men and children. Each of us is an individual. Yes, we belong to society and most of us enjoy being part of a group. I know I do.

However, I don't want people to assume that I am the one who does the cooking in my relationship, nor do I want my significant other to expect me to clean like a Domestic Goddess. The truth is, I hate housekeeping. I find it boring and repetitive. I have talent and skills. So why should I be everything to some or all people? My family, friends, and clients are much happier when I do what I love. A lot of the myths we learn in our youth are about undermining our confidence, encouraging our role-playing, and denying our essence.

I have my own list of myths that are indicative of my personal experiences and personality. No doubt you have your own list, as well.

Global

A woman needs to be pretty and nice.
A woman is the primary caregiver.
A woman needs to be neat and well put together.
A woman needs to be a good homemaker.

Cross Generational

It is a man's world.
A woman needs to be polite.
A woman should not refuse sex with her spouse.
A women needs to put everyone else first.
A woman needs a husband.
A woman needs to swallow her shame.
A woman needs to obey her husband.
A woman should have children.
Women can't make tough decisions.
Successful women are bitches.

And Cross Cultural

A woman needs to have a top degree.
A woman needs to be attractive.
A woman needs to be a perfect mom.
A woman needs to keep in shape.
A woman needs to entertain with style.
A woman should not show anger.
A woman does not need to worry about finances.
A woman needs to strive to be independent and strong.
Women are the weaker sex.
It's a woman's job to take care of the household.

Make a list of all your myths and maybe even think about where they came from. Examine them in the light of day. If a myth doesn't serve your purpose, set it free and create your own truths. Repeat your truths over and over until they become a habit you know to be true.

Myth   True or False   How can I turn this myth into a truth for me?

> "We're destined to become glorious butterflies, yet we persist in perceiving ourselves as caterpillars, opting for crawling the safer but less exciting ground, instead of allowing ourselves to take flight."
>
> --NAVA ATLAS

Seven Steps to Crumble the Myth

1. Awareness

The first step to claiming your space is awareness, understanding how much we as women have lived our lives based on mythology and the stories we believe. We are locked in this prison. We might not have been the ones who built the walls, but we often embrace it, we make the bars more secure. We hammer in the lines so straight, so sure, and we whip ourselves for not being better mothers, better cooks, and better lovers. As the mother, wife, and employee, we rush to rescue our children, our men, our boss, and the whole world. We hold our arms out so wide until they are heavy and tired—until we weep with exhaustion and emptiness. We long for an escape, but we can't tell anyone for fear of being "a bad mother" or a wicked woman. As women, we huddle in corners together, piling on top of one another, and often comfort ourselves by discrediting others. We belittle our own sex. We become the prison guards of our spaces, perpetuating the myths of our jailers.

If you don't have awareness, you cannot change. If you don't feel a deep aching need, the desire to find a little corner of sunshine for your soul, you probably wouldn't be reading this book. The knowing is the start— when you can look at yourself and know that something is missing and that only you can make the something that will change everything. It does take structure, and by chipping away for at least 10 to 30 minutes a day, you can begin the process that will open you up to connecting to your strength.

2. Choice

We choose what we want to believe and how we see life. We choose what opportunities to take. We choose hope or lack of it. We choose love. If we have awareness, we choose to love ourselves first. We choose to stop trying to change the world, and we choose to focus on bettering ourselves. If each person in the world changes one person—themselves—for the better—wouldn't this planet be incredible? We choose to see good in others. We choose to live our lives in fear or in courage. If you want to make a difference in your life, then choose to take charge of your mindset and your moments. Millionaires, women who break glass ceilings, arrive because they choose their goals.

3. Truth

Truth is an essential ingredient in the awareness and choice recipe; if you can't see what you need to change, then how can you grow? If you think that your life sucks because of the people in it, you are right. The only one who can change that perception is you. If you want to live a conscious life, you must be able to look yourself in the mirror, but unlike the wicked stepmother, you must be open to hearing the truth. Flying takes so much strength, courage, and belief. Life really is like a fairy tale—reality is based on belief. If you believe you can do it, you can. Nothing external, and that includes other people, can stop you if you know you can do it. So if you want to fly, you have to harden your protective shell. You have to get really friendly with truth—your fears, your weaknesses, and how to overcome whatever it is that is holding you back from flying.

4. Desire

Do you know what you want? Do you know what you really feel? Are you connected to your physical self?

Our bodies are transmitters of our souls, our inner selves. Our inner Sacred Spirit is very aware of what we want. She is not afraid. We have covered her up in so many layers of garments and embellishments in denial. We have created a kingdom of shame, so that we don't look upon our desires. We talk about desire as our base nature, or the animal in us, like it's a weakness. Desire is healthy and very natural for humans. We are part of the animal kingdom. Look at dogs and cats—why do we love them so? They are transparent. When they are happy, they wag their tails. When they are hungry, they run to their bowls. They are connected to their desires, and they don't have human walls of shame to bury themselves behind. Know what you want and how to ask for it. Don't worry about what others think or do. Be focused on your desires. Think about who you are under your layers of camouflage, and allow the real you to have a voice in your life.

5. Decision

Know what you really want—listen to your heart, not your head. Lock the rules out and let the real you stand up, even if it's a very small thing, like taking 10 minutes a day to read, or eating that juicy fig, having a long soak in the tub, walking in the park. Make a pact with yourself to honor that decision. If you decide to go back to school or get fit, work through your negatives and knock them down one by one.

My friend, Harriet, told me, "I had showered in the morning, and I took another shower in the afternoon, I'm in the shower, thinking to myself, 'Why haven't I done this before? Why haven't I taken a shower in the p.m. and pampered myself with the scrub?' And I thought to myself, 'I never did because I never gifted myself the time, even though it's something that I love, and I felt so good afterwards.'"

Give yourself the gift of not only recognizing an indulgence—an act of self-love—but also make the decision to DO it. One of the most difficult things for me is to stop thinking so much and just take action. I have learned from Baethe Davis that making a decision is the key. It doesn't matter which decision you take, as long as you make one. Not making a decision can be poisonous; the problem, pain, or fear doesn't go away—it grows bigger in the dark. If it feels right—if your body says yes—keep a decisive journal, find a decision buddy, or calendar, give yourself a finite time and declare!

6. Action

After the decision is made, you will feel like air has entered you soul and your caterpillar will start to rise. Power comes from intention, the decision that is made from instinct. All that is left is action. Taking action may involve some investigation—if you want to take a class or learn a new skill, you might need to research options or prices. Maybe you have limited resources—take the first step and ask people for help. The world is full of people waiting to help you. Let people know what you want. Very few people can read your mind. Make a list of your goals, and then use mind mapping or a list to explore your options in getting where you need to go. An incredible thing happens when you decide to take charge of your life no matter how small the step. The Universe delivers clues and the right people to aid you. Know that no one can propel you but yourself, and no one can stop you but yourself. Buts are not allowed in the action hall of an aware woman.

7. Celebration

Once you have taken action, your first baby steps, celebrate. Pluck some flowers from the garden and put them on your table. Drink a glass of bubbly. Eat a chocolate or reward yourself with a walk. Recognize that you have taken a huge step to kick myth into the forgotten corner; you have taken a giant leap for you. You are good enough, you are connecting to your inner Goddess, everyone should rejoice—a happy woman is fulfilled. We can all be better, do better, and laugh louder when we have the pulsating energy of being in control of our own lives, even if it's just one window in a dark house. With every step toward your growth, more windows will light up.

The truth is we have a choice. Yes, it is often buried under a pile of rubble. Finding the confidence we lost as young girls will make us worthy enough to soar, special enough to count, deserving enough to be selfish—to take time to nurture ourselves.

Let go of worrying about "the good opinion of others." Of course, we want to be decent, considerate human beings, and that is desirable. I think most of us have an innate sense of decency and fairness. Recognizing that in others is often easy. Do you recognize the good in you? First, we have to see the value of our own opinions and wants before we begin to look abroad. Sometimes the only myth we need to let go of is guilt.

Women have been taught that, for us, the earth is flat, and that if we venture out, we will fall off the edge.

~ANDREA DWORKIN

Myths are ideas and concepts that other people have used against us, or that we have used against ourselves to stop us from eating the banana. Don't hold onto a myth just because it came before you.

You can be whom you desire if first you master your myths.

1) Know your myths. List all the myths that hold your feet to the ground.

2) Let go of what no longer serves you.

3) Rewrite the rules – your life, your truths.

4) Give yourself permission to take time for yourself.

SELFISH ACTION:

Find Your Color to Banish Myth

Find the color that makes you feel happy—try one of these activities to get your color juices flowing.

- What color do you choose when you get a manicure?
- Visit the paint store to check out a chip.
- Open your closet and look for your favorite scarf.
- Take a stroll to some stores that excite you.
- Walk down the garden path. Nature is full of surprising colors and combinations.
- Get on the Internet and check out an inspiring fashion blog, like Sartorialist, which can be found at: http://www.thesartorialist.blogspot.com/

You can bring in this favorite color in a tiny way with a little dish or go wild and paint a wall or a whole room. Drapes are a great way to bring in a big punch without painting. If all your furniture is pretty basic and boring, color in a pillow or a rug will brighten up your room.

CHAPTER TWO

Celebrate Selfish

"NO NEED TO HURRY. NO NEED TO SPARKLE.
NO NEED TO BE ANYBODY BUT ONESELF."
— *Virginia Woolf, (A Room of One's Own* and *Three Guineas)*

Now that we've covered myths, let's move into how to claim your self.

It is past time to be selfish. To embrace your space, claim your personal selfish room. A room of your own, just as Virginia Woolf wrote.

A very exclusive selfish club of one: Welcome.

Why do I say selfish?

The ultimate meaning of being selfish is to give the luxury of thought to self. Be who you are under the layers of jobs that you have taken or been given, where no one is watching and no one is asking. Claim time to connect to your depth.

Learn to love, honor, and value yourself.

Ignite your Selfhood—the island within—and it all starts with choice.

Choose to connect to your inner Divine, the beast within. I laugh to myself because I believe that Beauty and the Beast were one. None of us can be all sunshine and roses. There are thorns. We need to get comfortable with the thorns.

To get very intimate with the underbelly of whom we are so that our beast can be mellow and roll in the grass, not kept locked in the dungeon of our consciousness, so we live in fear of showing our true selves.

Let's get comfortable and be nobody but ourselves, just as Woolf encourages. Of course, we need to know ourselves to get comfortable. In Chapter One, I talked about myth and letting go. You have to peel back the layers and separate yourself from other people's expectations and walls. Quit worrying about being liked or feeling guilty because you don't spend all day with the kids; there is no such thing as universal approval, so you may as well please the one that counts the most—you. There is a very good reason for not spending more time with your kids. Acknowledge that, fix what needs fixing, and move on. Own the life skills your kids are learning from you.

Stop apologizing. Stop saying yes to everyone and everything. Start saying no to whatever you either want to or can give up. Saying yes to you is your number one priority. Your family needs you to be whole, happy, and connected.

Virginia Woolf's quote really says it all. Honoring one's true self is the most precious belief we can hold for ourselves and, indeed, everyone we know. Stop thinking other people are better because they go faster, they shine brighter, or they look more put together. We are glorious as we are. By denying our true nature, we deny our very fiber. We cut off our own blood flow to our souls, our Divine Spirit.

Each of us is a unique individual, with talents and natures that belong to us. We need to celebrate that individual. Nurture that inner child, just as we would any beloved child in our life. We need to be kind to us.

We are constantly being encouraged to be true to ourselves, while at the same time being found to be wanting, with familiar remarks like, "Oh! She is so untidy; she is so loud."

Really, what other people are is who they are—just the way they are. If they are fumbling in the dark and have lost their way, it is because so much of society has been raising each other with the concept of conformity. The fumbling is from their lack of belief in themselves.

We enjoy the first years of our lives in joy and wonder—everything is new and possible. When we get to our teen years, we are suddenly so bottled up in fears of all "the mistakes" we will make, being twisted into a pretzel with all the mixed messages and commands to squeeze our round selves into a square peg. We are told smart girls aren't glamorous. And what do we do to become "popular?" We lose our connection with ourselves and become the other, almost as if we were ashamed of our true selves. We attempt to make "I" disappear in the crowd, becoming invisible, bonded in servitude to shoulds, musts, and the desires of others and the myths they perpetuate.

> *"Selfish has gotten a bad rap. We've been conditioned to think being selfish is unkind and hurtful to others. The truth is that being selfish is the opportunity to be your 100% authentic self and to take care of your own needs and desires. It's taking responsibility for you, who you are, and who you want to be. When we are our true and authentic selves, we are practicing a selfishness that allows us to BE, while we are kind and generous with others. When you take the time to be kind and generous with yourself, the natural outgrowth is being kind and generous with all those you encounter!*

> Lauren Shelby
> *Interior Designer Spaces Within*
> http://spaceswithin.com

I think as women we are often trained from birth to help others—to pick up after other people, turn the other cheek when we are hurt and hide our feelings.

We are constantly told to keep quiet, not to make noise, to silently sweep as we weep.

At the same time, we are encouraged to be creatures of perfumed beauty—to be desirable, yet not too desirable that we are "asking for it," to look good, but not get embroiled in too much emotion.

We are persuaded to create the persona of perfect mother, a sex kitten in the bedroom, a goddess in the kitchen, a tiger without claws in the boardroom.

We are groomed not to complain or make waves—to be all things to everyone in our lives, while completely disregarding who we are—taking out the self, like so much trash. Trained to refute the terrible sin of "being selfish," we punish women for daring to pull to their light. So we try to be the perfect Cinderella girl who can go from sweeping ashes and kissing asses to being the lady of the manor in one fell swoop, with grace, style, and not a moment's pause. What is so fascinating in all those fairy tales is that the change that freed the princess was all through a woman! She birthed freedom to be caged in someone else's dream.

In creating a creature that looks good is cheerful, supportive, and has no personal needs, Barbie is born. They are all the reflection of the world around us.

It's interesting how life or the Universe prods and kicks us to get our attention. Finally, after ignoring all the signs, we are bitch slapped so hard, we can still hear the ringing long after the last bell has subsided.

All this stuff is not real. That is the kicker. For most of us, no one but us can stop us from showing up as ourselves. We don't have to give up before we reach our goals.

We do, however, have to adopt a new mindset. I have a name for it: Big Ass Hair Do Attitude.

BAH do A

This means is that many of us may have big, messy, untidy hair—voluptuous, in your face, real hair, or other big, bold body parts. We may have big breasts or big bums, or we may have an attitude that some people find too loud.

Do you know what I'm saying? Embrace your Big Ass Hair, do it. Walk the walk and ignore the naysayers. Don't play in their playground. Instead, invite them to play in yours. When they put you down for being too feminine, too masculine, or for being a dumb female, don't walk, baby, do the wiggle, your way. Flip that hair, embrace your deep, real inner woman.

Stop wasting breath to convince people with words and take a leap into molding your possibilities by walking around the walls. We don't need to break through glass ceilings; we can take the stairs anytime we really want—and in high heels! As women, I want us to stop lying down, unless we are in the mood. Let's give up trying to make it so hard. Remember another person's put down is just opinion—overrated hot air bubbles that have very little power over us, unless we allow it.

Claim your BIG ASS HAIR and Do

Part of claiming your Big Ass Hair and Do Attitude is to listen to your body, your inner voice. She is a barometer for what is going on for you at your deepest level.

Sharon Jakubey has taught me about listening to my body.

Your body and you are a team, working together. Without your body and senses, you can barely lift your head above the pillow—you can scarcely draw a breath. You need her, and she needs you. Your constant companion, from day one to your deathbed, she signals when you need a break, protects soft parts, cradles your thoughts and feelings, warns you of danger, and allows you joy in movement. She knows all about your Big Ass Hair Do.

Paying attention to your body is as necessary as breathing. Don't worry about breathing.

Your body breathes for you, but you do need to remember NOT TO HOLD YOUR BREATH.

I asked Sharon Jakubecy to share some selfish tips and insight:

"Many women grapple with their own sense of confidence and body image. There is a common belief that if they lack confidence, it is because there is something wrong with them. When they feel insecure, anxious, or uncomfortable in their own skin, they are actually interfering with their bodies own natural design by:

- *Tightening their neck and shoulder muscles,*
- *Pulling their ribcage forward,*
- *Squeezing their arms in toward their ribs,*
- *Compressing their diaphragm, and*
- *Generally, making it impossible to BREATHE.*

When they physically cannot breathe, they will necessarily feel nervous, anxious, uncomfortable, insecure, and unattractive. Feeling so uncomfortable, women will then disconnect from their own bodies, get entrenched with their thoughts, and lose any sense of grounding.

When you are feeling overwhelmed, anxious, or unattractive, take some time to listen to your body. Notice the position you are holding yourself in and if you are interfering with the natural, easy flow of breath. Then, gently, slowly, and kindly, UNDO tight muscles. Return to your dynamic open and tall posture. Soften. When you change how you move and use less tension, you can connect to yourself, your body, and your breath.

Releasing old, harmful tension allows your spine to lengthen and your chest to widen. Your ribs "dance" with your breath and continually move with every inhale and exhale. Your shoulders soften away from your ears. Your entire body is long, and your posture is dynamic! Releasing all the compressing tension changes your emotional state, as well. Since your body can move with your breath, you feel fearless, grounded, and sexy!"

Sharon Jakubecy, Your Personal Director, Certified Alexander Technique teacher. To find out more

about Sharon and her services, please visit
www.SharonJakubecy.com.

Give yourself breathing room to take stock and realize
how much of this pain from running the endurance marathon
of life, pretty much without a compass, has been about
holding in breath. All the people are pointing fingers, all
shouting in voices, living in the Tower of Babel – you did this
wrong! Can you help me? Carry my load, fix my pain, make
this work, shut up, go here, follow my instructions, stand up
straight, don't listen to your heart, stupid, don't laugh so
loud...blah blah, fill in the blank_____. What
have they asked of you over and over?

Give yourself permission to let go of the outside world
for a short period every day and putter around in tranquility.
Commune with your inner goddess. Connect to peace on
earth. If we all connect to our inner heart and listen, the
world itself will slow so it can breathe out. When we
approach life at our full power, in love with life and those
who inhabit it, guilt free and without anxiety, we can change
our world and the world.

I am in gratitude for all the blessings on the road of my
life—all the rest stops that nourished me, made me laugh, and
filled my soul with oxygen. It has been quite a trip. I know I
am not done yet. When I was younger, I wanted it all to be
over sooner. Now, I am delighted to be traveling this road
with you—boon companions, receiving lessons and glory. I
feel sheer happiness for how much we are responsible for
what happens to ourselves, for rose petals that fall from the
sky, and the way our body and mind sleep curled into each
other at night, satisfied after a day of joyful quest.

What are you in gratitude for? Sometimes it takes a
spiritual retreat to remember the good in life.

Many of life lessons come through friendship and the
human interaction expectations and demands that we hold. In
the end, we all want similar things—recognition, trust,

certainty, acceptance, love, first to yourself and then to those you nourish.

We cannot call on those in our circle to save us, to bring us joy as if it were a tray of food. We each need to sit at the banquet of life and feast and pay our dues. No one else can eat for us.

Many women are raised with the idea that serving self or being selfish is a cardinal sin. We are raised as vessels to serve, a container to hold the world filled with others' needs, wants, and desires. Without barriers or boundaries, we have elastic lives that change shape, and we learn to please.

You need to give yourself all that you long to give those around you. **First.**

Refocus on what it takes to enable you to lead a better life.

Rediscover that little girl, and reconnect with your inner Divine.

The Selfish Check Rules

How many rules can you say yes to?

Renew who you are. Reflect and grow.
Stop. Listen to your body.
Yes to no.
Yes to letting go of other people's baggage.
Yes to helping others learn to fish.
No to humoring anger.
Yes to owning your responsibility and no one else's.
Stop drinking other people's Kool Aid.
Yes to your needs.
Stop swallowing self-doubt, low self-worth, holding in the pain, holding back the tears.
Stop hiding the hurt.
Stop apologizing to the people in your life.
Yes to Big Ass Hair Do Attitude.
Yes to selfish time.
Yes to no guilt for doing what we are born to do.

Yes to no shame.

Yes to acknowledging your skills and talents and following your path.

Yes to trust and love for yourself first.

We cannot help the world around us if we do not have a strong foundation. We cannot be a steady rock for our partner or a holding space for our children if the well is dry.

Take time away to chill in your cocoon. Take care of your body mind and heart.

Be at peace with your inner being.

Fiona Stolze told me, "I would love to have a beautiful, nurturing cocoon to retreat to, a space just for me to be in, meditate in...I like the word cocoon, She-Lair. I can't change or hugely serve the world by being out there doing things for others. By being that change and completely nurturing myself, that is the inspiration for others. Time for giving myself much more permission to have the goodies in life and be the goddess I am. That's a full-time job, and it's not selfish."

> - Make a list of all the things you do for love of you.
> - Make a list of all the things you do for love of others.
> - List all the times you have put others before you.
> - How does your list look, and what does it make you feel?
>
> Make a commitment in writing, stating how much time you are going to give yourself daily to reconnect with the real you. These topics can get you started journaling on your journey to discovery.

*Every time you state what you want or believe,
you're the first to hear it. It's a message to both
you and others about what you think is possible.
Don't put a ceiling on yourself.*

~ OPRAH WINFREY, *O MAGAZINE*, DECEMBER 2003

Successful women in life and in business are people who just do it. They have a need, and they follow their intuition.

They don't solicit other people's opinions. They certainly get help. They find the best coaches. Every woman who has risen to the top did so because she broke the myths and took the stairs. They believed, set goals, perspired, found their space, and nurtured the star of brilliance within.

It is simple, not easy, and you may not desire fame or fortune. Find your path.

Brandy Mychals, Creator of the Character Code System™, told me:

"As a Class President Character Code, it would be very easy for me to just get the work done and focus on the tasks. We tend to be a little in our 'heads' and forget the rest of the body that is attached. What I know to be true, though, is that I have to honor my body and my needs for nourishment, rest, and play. So, I just plan for it and make sure I don't miss it. As a result, I experience more joy throughout the journey and don't have to worry about burnout because I maintain clear boundaries. Life isn't all about work. Love yourself and those around you. Take time for yourself!"

How does a woman learn to be selfish?

She makes a space and carves out time to indulge the connection, using tools like journaling.

My own personal experience of growth and transition made me realize that it's hard to know who you are if you don't take time to get to the core of yourself. I have had countless hours of self-discovery, journaling about why I made certain decisions and figuring out what happened to my inner child, that little girl that had stars in her eyes and laughter in her heart.

Play your life awake and 100% engaged, understanding the stakes and diving in.

Start with your journey and the lessons you learned.

Explore if any particular event stood out or if you ever make decisions based on your gut feelings, and how that worked out.

It's a myth that caring for others is a woman's role—not all women want to be caretakers. Not every mother is an ideal parent or a perfect lover. Malcolm Gladwell said we need 10 years to become an expert at anything. I think that includes caretaking in all its forms. Desire plays an important part of the equation. No one learns much unless they are motivated. I have worked with people who have been doing the same job for 20 years, and their level of expertise has not increased. It takes curiosity to turn a job into a passion or a growth opportunity. You are an opportunity. If you have any curiosity about who you are or what you could become, you need to nurture the flame. No one can grow without nutrients and oxygen.

An adult needs to make their own decisions, children need to learn to make their own decisions, and we all need to be prepared to accept the consequences. I believe in embracing the family and doing things with and for each other as a community, out of love and respect. Being selfish is something we need to put into the equation so that when we have to tell people no, we can do it with the conviction it deserves.

You can still take time to take care of your family, but you have to create boundaries. You are a stronger person when you take time for yourself—when you let people know that you count. The family needs to understand that this is your uninterrupted time. If you respect yourself, your family members will respect you. If you put yourself last every time an opportunity comes up—like taking the smallest bit of food because there is not enough, or you constantly negate your importance by your actions—you are essentially teaching your family that you don't count. You are worth exactly what you show you are worth. That doesn't mean you shouldn't help others or teach your kids to be generous or giving. These are noble lessons in which the whole family should partake. You are not the sacrificial lamb. Each individual is equally important.

Early Warning Signs

When my daughter was 12 years old, she told me, "You know, Mum, you're one of those people that if you were in an airplane and the airplane was going to crash, you would be taking that oxygen mask and putting it on the person next to you, you wouldn't even put it on yourself." That was a real awakening for me because she was only 12 and telling her mother, who was close to 50, that she doesn't have much self-respect, that she can't take care of herself, because when you're on a plane, if you don't put that mask on yourself first, you can't help anyone else. So, that's the rule of life. You've got to help yourself first. Surround yourself with good things, clear boundaries, people who understand your boundaries, and you'll be a lot stronger. You won't be just a survivor; you'll be a person who steers her life—a woman who will be able to deal with anything that comes up, even a plane crash.

That's the essential essence of loving yourself. You can't be anything to anyone if you are not true to yourself. I think being selfish is essential. Everyone wins because you can be a healthy person who fulfills your needs, wants, and desires, without feeling guilty about that. When you are happy or content, it is so much easier to be a willing participant in the lives of those around you. So saying yes to you is the first step to healthy relationships and lifelong happiness.

No one else can make you happy. Only you can make yourself happy. Only you can flame the fires of your dreams. You can't make anyone else happy, either. Each of us is responsible for ourselves. That is a universal truth.

Whenever you compromise to make someone else happy, what happens? They still aren't happy because they want it all their own way, and the result is a bunch of unhappy people.

If you let other people decide for you, they are not going to choose what you want—they don't know what you want. So everyone goes home mad, sad, or disappointed.

Choose what you want, or take turns so each one has a turn being happy. Compromise is the kiss of death. I remember years ago when my husband and I went out to choose our first couch. We had completely different tastes.

We both compromised so much on a very expensive piece of furniture that, even to this day, when I think about that couch, I am revolted by what we settled for. I could not wait to get rid of something that should have been a purchase of joy, all because of compromise. Compromise costs money. We had to replace a perfectly good couch that neither of us liked. I always tell my clients you can compromise on love (if you want) but never compromise on a couch.

What is it about compromise that you can't let go of?

The No Compromise Rule

I created my own No Compromise rule, and wrote it down so I can see it daily.

I cobbled together my most important values for how I want to live my life from now on.

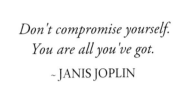

Don't compromise yourself.
You are all you've got.

~ JANIS JOPLIN

My No Compromise Rule is based on not settling for less. That means that I know what I want. I accept responsibility as soon as possible. I take what I want, and I acknowledge my gifts.

I love myself as is.

I don't hide behind lies.

I am free to improve myself—no waiting for someday.

If I miss out, no whining is allowed.

I don't accept responsibility for other people's opinions, feelings, or disappointments. I am not allowed to wallow in guilt or shame.

I don't apologize for who I am, and I shut my inner meanie up.

I take time for myself, and I pay myself first.

I celebrate my body. I have a Big Ass Hair Do Attitude.

Take some time to compose your own No Compromise Rule. What values do you want to live by? What do you need to do to bring out your inner woman? Don't forget your Big Ass Hair Do.

Are you compromising on your surroundings?

Create surroundings that enhance you.

Are you settling for how your furniture lands?

Take control of your room.

You can create your own cocoon. Your own retreat is waiting for you.

Single and guilty?

When you've been through a bad relationship and you're single and raising kids, often you focus solely on your children. This is a key time for you. Ten to twenty minutes to yourself a day will benefit your children. They will learn that women/mothers take time to honor herself because she is important, and you will have the mental resources to deal with any needs they have. It's much better to spend a little less time with your family, rather than being frazzled and preoccupied all day long.

"Surprise...I'm completely comfortable being selfish. I know that I'm so much better when I'm taking care of myself. When I was single, I wasn't sure I would have kids because I didn't want to be the 'Super Mom' my mom had to be when I was growing up. I knew I would have to find a man that wanted to participate in bringing up kids or I wouldn't have any. Lucky me, I found Stu." Darcie Newton

12 Steps to Self- IS-H

1. Clarity. We need clarity to be selfish, to hone in on who we are as a person and what we want. It's our space, things, and memories, and we should be comfortable reflecting that in our Cocoon and our homes.

2. Focus. It is really important to take your 30 minutes a day in a space where you can concentrate with no distractions.

3. Acceptance. Recognize your gifts, connect with your passion, and enjoy it.

4. Time. We tend to give time away or say we never have enough time; we need to take that time for ourselves. Embrace that selfish feeling.

5. Celebrate yourself. Whether you want to have your nails done or go into your fabulous room and lie down and eat

chocolates, you deserve the reminder of how wonderful you are.

6. Meditation. I think it means different things to different people. What is your body and your intuition telling you? Think about nothing; quiet your mind, stop all that monkey chatter that goes on. Dream and be in that subconscious state of being, step out of distractions.

7. Recognition. This is about you, recognize who you are. Enjoy reflections, memories, and the layering that your possessions create in your life.

8. Power of letting go. In things we don't have any control of, let go. Take control of what is yours. That's part of claiming your power—releasing other people's problems.

9. Resources. Build up plenty of resources. Ask for help. And take it. You need support.

10. Self Love. Do you love yourself? Accept yourself as fabulous? You should.

11. Choice. Make decisions that serve you. You can and should decide for you. Don't let the outside world or anyone in it take that power from you.

12. Listen to your kinetic sense get in touch with your body. Listen to what your body is saying.

"Thinking of my own selfish place, I am thinking of a place where I can have my own little secrets that I do not wish to share with anyone—something that is truly just mine. I am talking about my imaginary secrets, secrets from the past, dreams, dream castles and much more. I would hide stuff there, make it interesting for others to explore and find stuff (where, in the end, it's just my imagination that records everything) and nobody can find anything if they'd look."
Franziska san Pedro http://franziskasanpedro.com/

So how do we work and live with intention? As I have mentioned before, it's about making a determination that you want to do something and living your life the way you plan it or decide it. Don't fall into things because they're there, if that's not what suits you. Sometimes, things happen around you because you want it. You set the intention, do something, and then suddenly you realize that all this stuff around you is falling into place to help you along because of intention. The principle is the same in your workspace. If you want it to look serene, set the intention. To have a place that you can go to for a personal break, set that intention. Maybe right now, you do something that you hate, but that doesn't mean you have to stay in that place. You're not locked there. There is an escape, maybe not this minute, but there will be, and it's the same in your home. Just because everything around you looks drab and depressing, it doesn't mean it has to stay that way. Set the intention and take the first tiny step. In a room, start with one drawer and spend ten minutes a day clearing it out until you are done, then move to the next drawer or the next space. Or start keeping a journal, jotting down three pages of a free flow of consciousness daily, no matter how trivial. It could be your laundry list. It is starting the ball rolling that moves you toward change. What intention are you planning to set?

After reading some of my blogs about the power of personal space, Louise felt the need to create her own Sacred Space. Her husband got involved, too, finding her the perfect chair while she was out of town as a surprise:

> *"A huge part of the messages I'm getting from all these readings I'm doing—that I have to serve myself before I can serve others—that I have always served others without serving myself, and that leads to resentments. No More! I HAVE to be selfish to fulfill my purpose in life. I am creating my hideaway, and my picture from Franzisko San Pedro will be part of that... It was in my chart that I wouldn't really figure this out till the second half of my life, so there we have it.*

Luckily, I have a man that wants to participate, too—looking back, it's me that's shut him out of that, rather than the other way around."
Louise Edington http://louiseedington.com/

This is about honoring that inner you and loving her, accepting her, warts and all. No one has checked wobbly cottage cheese thighs on their wish list. Yet so many of us have them. Should we continue to buy into a perfect world that doesn't exist? Or shall we just fling worry and remorse about our body shapes and hair imperfections to the wind, knowing each of us is beautiful in our own right? Each of us deserves our cozy cocoon in the sun—that warm feeling of being loved for who we are, exactly as we are. We are a package deal. This is not like a restaurant where we get to say, "Dressing on the side and no onions." Yes, we can choose to improve our wobbly bits or learn skills, and ultimately, that is our greatest gift—to choose and be able to say no when we mean it, and yes to an opportunity we are excited about. Truly, this is what separates us from caterpillars. We can turn our legs into wings by setting boundaries and goals, creating what we want in our lives, and claiming our goals and our Big Ass Hair Do.

> *"I have an everyday religion that works for me. Love yourself first, and everything else falls into line."*
>
> - LUCILLE BALL

Demanding lifestyles are eased when you yourself feel refreshed and relaxed from your mental "Spa."
Time alone is so powerful for organizing thoughts, relaxing your mind, and "de-frazzling." The process is so

enriching on a daily basis it becomes addictive and changes your life and everyone in it, for the better. People respond to how you act. A calm strong woman gets a completely different response than an overworked, anxious woman.

Studies show that spending time alone is very beneficial. Alone time allows us to connect with our creativity to resolve problems and gain inner strength. We glow, and people are attracted to the power energy that we release. Author and philosopher Mark Vernon says that if we don't love ourselves, we can't do anything of value for other people, and the irony is that by being alone, gaining connection and confidence, we become very appealing to other people.

Sounds like a reason to run to my Chic Cocoon.

I have mentioned that I have spent a great deal of my life living to the tune of other people's needs. Until my crisis, I hardly spared a moment thinking about who I was and what I wanted. Starting the process made me realize I have to know who I am to live it.

We need to find a room, a sacred room, a space to call our own where we go in, lock the door, and spend quality time with ourselves. It's a place where we reconnect with our inner goddess, find out who we are through journaling, or through just doing whatever it is that we want in a room of our own. So many of us are so busy that we're running on the hamster wheel. We never stop to think what we need to do and ask ourselves, "How can I change this? How can I stop myself from feeling so crazy?" This is the first step, taking oneself out into one's own space, finding quiet time within one's head.

Not everyone wants to do things from a big stage. No matter how simple your goals are, if you want to achieve them, if you want to be recognized, first you must know who you are. You cannot be whole without unlearning many of the lessons or myths you carry with you.

Start creating boundaries, and what better boundary than a room with walls and a door with a key?

7 Boundary Builders - A Bridge to Happiness

1. Set your personal time into your daily routine for a time when you are alone (lunchtime/ after breakfast/ pre family wake up)

2. Teach your children and spouse that a woman has needs that can only be met alone.

3. Every day, set an appointment with yourself when you will be unavailable for anything (except extreme emergencies).

4. Dial into dreams—work on goals and milestones

5. Celebrate "Happy Hour" for one – this is all about your moment.

6. Indicate you need a time out with a sign or a code.

7. Use the naptime/walk/ weeding—that no one else wants to do excuse.

Are selfish people happier? Definitely, and people who are aware of self are more successful. Being "selfish" means setting boundaries.

Key for successful women is the time they take to regroup. Focusing on their needs enables clear, concise actions. It is difficult to achieve greatness when your thoughts are scattered and your power is in pieces. Build yourself up alone in your space. Quiet your mind and your surroundings. Indulge in a luxury. Reward yourself, and that reward will gift your loved ones.

Embarrassed to claim your own space?

Many times, we feel uncomfortable or embarrassed to admit that we need to have downtime or escape, or that we are struggling from overwhelm. I think being vulnerable is so powerful and freeing. Take what you need; remember the No Compromise Rule.

As soon as you realize how wonderful this makes you feel, other people's opinions will no longer matter. It is okay to admit when something feels good, even though you may feel uncomfortable in the beginning.

We have to be strong in our pursuit of happiness. It takes work, and we have to own it, right? Own our passion, move forward, and hey, embrace our big selves. Our rules rock!

Many of us have been trained to feel guilty about taking personal time or being selfish. I've seen women who often make a point that they are not selfish. They take pride in taking a back seat. I think that is so sad. To deny themselves a bit of pleasure, like the biggest piece of pie for once, is selfish in a bad way to me. It is being a martyr and trying to make everyone else feel bad because you made a sacrifice. Time alone is a boon; it's your space and your freedom to fill up the concentration of who you are, so that for the rest of the day, it's okay that it is being diluted.

We all need downtime. We all need to celebrate our inner child, dance in the room, or just do something crazy just because it gives us such a sense of pleasure and release.

Know that you are like a rubber band, and if you don't stop and relax, you will just keep stretching and snap. Even though you may be alone all day, you're not taking "you" time, so it is essential to consciously put down the tools and move into that space. That's very different. You can't be on all the time. It's just exhausting to maintain, and you can't maintain an even temper. Life just gets too crazy when you don't take time to be you in your Selfish Space. You're honoring the self in this. It's not like you are dropping responsibility and running away. You are being responsible because taking the time to connect with your self is very healthy for everyone in your life.

Many women get up early in the morning so they can be alone in the home. I love to awaken early, drink in the dawn, sip tea, and write in my journal with a clear head.

You don't have to do it at 5:30. You can do it at 12:30 or 9:30 in the evening.

You decide what works for you and what feels good to you. That is the beauty of it. It's individual. You're not going to do it if it feels too hard or too demanding. You choose what you want to do. Pick your passion and treat yourself to a daily dose.

Many times when we are part of a unit, we do things because other people ask us to, and we don't really think about what matters to us. We don't think of ourselves as separate. The time in your room, in your space, is about you. Get in the habit of focusing on your needs only. Do things in your time that feed your soul, not things that drag you down. Make sure it's a selfish need, not connected to anyone or anything else, and that there is no obligation; it must be pure pleasure or self-discovery.

What do I do if my husband doesn't support my need for space?

That's a tough one. You have to fight for your space and your rights. I don't mean fisticuffs or anything like that, but stand firm if you can. Maybe you can go ahead and do your thing without telling your significant other until you build up the courage. While I don't advocate living a lie, I do think sometimes omission can work well until you are comfortable enough to be open. In a normal healthy relationship, you should be able to tell your partner that you're doing something, whether they respect it or not. It's okay to not have the approval of your spouse to do what you want to do, as long as you are not putting yourself in danger. You may not approve of him sitting in front of the couch drinking beer and watching sports, but he does it. So it's the same thing. It's allowing; he has to give you the respect to allow you to do what you want, and you have to let him know that this is not negotiable. You might win his respect and approval, especially when he sees the advantages of what happens when you're so much more grounded and so much more in tune and available the rest of the time. I think it can be advantageous for your sex life, too.

How exciting would it be to have him get involved in encouraging you to get selfish?

"Honey, where can I move this chair for you?" might be the response. Visualizing the response you want can't hurt. In fact, that might be a great journal or vision board exercise.

Find a way to connect, turn them on, and when I say that, I mean in both ways. Whatever gets them involved and makes them want to assist you helps the two of you and the whole family dynamic.

> You can share the mutual advantages of Chic Cocoon. Claim your free 7 Selfish Sex Tips report on my website www.chiccocoon. com/selfishspaces bodytips

It's such a simple request, really, and such a necessary endeavor.

If you have a partner, from this moment forth, set rules for what you expect from your relationship. If you don't set your intentions, how can you complain if people walk all over you? Are you a mat or a woman?

The key here is that we often allow baggage into our lives. Maybe we've had bad lessons, I know I have. We cannot let people walk all over us, even our husbands or partners. That's a hard lesson that may take a lot of practice and re-reading of our No-Compromise Rule. We set the boundaries ourselves, and we have to demand that we get that space and be okay with their disapproval, with having a different opinion. This doesn't have to be about anger at all; it's about respect. Sharing respect frees us up in a million ways, so we don't have to keep silent for the sake of peace. So much joy comes into every part of our lives when we're comfortable with being ourselves.

Behavioral memory muscles—we all have them; they go back in the same positions if we don't massage the muscles.

Response is habit. You have to actively want to change the patterns in order to change your life. If you want growth and honesty, you have to go through the uncomfortable part of changing habits. It's like going to the chiropractor and having your bones moved and then having the muscles massaged into new patterns. Now the muscles are in the right place, but that can be painful—it takes quite a bit of adjusting.

Your selfish move:

Set your boundaries. Only you can build the wall. Say no. Practice saying no. Practice building your wall; you need protection. We all do. Do it today. Say no to someone else. Say yes to you.

Teaching our nearest and dearest to respect our boundaries and their own should be on our top 10 list of life skills.

If you mother-in-law or (fill in the blank) _____ refuses to respect your rules, you have to go back to your rulebook. When a puppy pees inside, what do you do?

You put her outside. You are teaching her your rules. People are like puppies—they need guidance.

The best way to teach others your rules is to develop your own boundary book and keep it sacred. Children learn by example, not by word.

Women have a lot of issues around boundaries, all tied up with self-worth /myths we learned as young girls. (See Chapter 1, From Myth to Mastery)

We put ourselves last, which is a cardinal sin in my book.

No one will respect us in the morning or another time of day if we don't respect ourselves. Sleeping with a man on the first date is not the issue. The issue is was that a boundary of yours that you stepped over?

People fail to understand this stuff until they learn that it's okay for other people to do things or that it's okay for them not to do what you want them to do, immediately or ever. You can't make people do stuff. Well, you can coerce people that are weaker than you, but that is no fun. Is that what you want to teach your kids?

Each of us has our own rulebook, and the cool thing is we make those rules. The tough part is that we need to own those rules and own the consequences of breaking the rules. So if you set a boundary and you give someone permission to break it, that is your responsibility. (I am not talking about when people break rules of life through anger and violence— that is a whole different subject that is not addressed in this book.) I am talking about normal relationship dynamics and you allowing someone to step over the fence. A couple years before I got divorced, I used to cook, work on my business at home, plus shop and take care of my daughter. I decided to stop cooking. It took too much time, and I wasn't enjoying it. It became expendable. My ex is an excellent cook, so he started shopping and cooking. I decided that since he cared more than I did about what we ate, that should become his responsibility. I have since discovered that there are a lot of women whose husbands do the cooking. I love that skill in a man.

Respect your kids/spouse/in-laws and let them know your boundaries are law, by deed.

Keep in mind the airplane and mask scenario; you can't help anyone else, UNLESS you help yourself first. If you don't take the time for you, you can't be there in a meaningful way for your children. Everyone knows when you show up with your body, but not in spirit. At my daughter's graduation, I snapped at a relative, who became infuriated. I could have let that dictate my mood and ruin a very important celebration, but I apologized profusely and decided to just let go of any guilt or responsibility and kept my happiness factor on float. I wanted to be there for my daughter in her moment, and I was in 100% enjoyment. That is power, and every day, you have the choice to focus on what you want to feel daily. It all starts with boundaries.

Explain to your children that your happiness depends on having time to yourself, and getting what they need from you is directly linked. Kids are great about understanding things, and they're much more forgiving than adults. They don't pass judgment or feel like it's their fault because you want time for yourself. They feel good about it. "I'm doing it so I can help myself and be there for you when you need me." When a kid feels overwhelmed, they go into their rooms and take some quiet time. That timeout is really a gift in a sense because it gives them a moment to calm down and come back to themselves. We don't want to constantly fall out or fall over ourselves in front of other people. That is more than most people need or want.

No whining! If you choose to do something—you felt like a quiet night inn and your spouse talked you into going out—that is your choice and your responsibility. Jump in and do it 100% or just say no.

People treat us how we expect to be treated. What are your expectations? What signals are you giving? It is actually true <gasp> that other people—not just our spouses—cannot read our minds. If you want something, speak up. Refuse what you don't want or don't need.

My mother-in-law (daughter/ friend, etc.) barges into my room whenever she wants.

There are many family members or friends that think that you belong to them, and it's essential to set your rules. Everything in life has rules. Make sure that your life is run on your rules. You come first. You need to pay yourself first. You are the fortress in your life. Take care of the fortress. Keep it in good repair. Let the moat down when needed and pull it back up when needed.

Be honest. Be steadfast. Focus on your need. Know why you are setting that particular boundary. And then tell the fence jumper that the rules are in charge. Sit down and have a talk with them, explaining that this is the way it is, that they cannot barge in. They're not allowed to just show up, or whatever your rule is that they are violating. The worst-case scenario is that you have to get a lock and a key and make sure no one else has a key to that room. Then you can lock yourself in. Nobody gets in without your permission. You need to accept how important it is to claim your space and stand on it, just like a dog with their territory—they piss around the circle so you know that they've been there and that the space is theirs.

List your territory-marking manifesto—everything that is essential for creating Your Own Book of Rules.

This is your life. Take charge of your rulebook (throw out myths and musts).

Non-negotiable	Negotiable	Free

Selfhood Rules

In order to connect with your self, you need to establish your personal rules for living.

Write down your list of absolutes you want to run your life by.

What is important to your Big Self, Your She – center, what do you need?

What you are willing to negotiate?

What you not willing to give up or compromise on?

Make a list with three columns.

Your absolutes/ your negotiables/ your not at alls.

Absolutes	Negotiables	Not at Alls

When you're an adult, how weird is it that you have to share a room? That's kind of crazy when you think about it. When you're a child, you get your own room, but when you're an adult, oh no, you don't get your own room. You have to share it.

What is perception, really?

It's not real because it's perception, right? We create our own realities. We craft our world out of perception. So perception is reality. In many ways, we create the issues that repeat within our lives, and then we assume they are impossible to fix.

We look at our problems and think there's no way we can do this differently. It's just like looking at a room and thinking there's no way to move these pieces and make the room look different because it's never going to work.

I have discovered that we just need to jump in, just decide to do it, and miraculously it works. When I do a room rearrangement, I don't plan it.

I have no idea what I'm going to do when I get there because I don't know what needs to be done until I am physically moving the room around. I don't let myself pre-plan it. It sets up all these pre-conceived ideas and blocks out any chance to be surprised by creating something amazing. When you go into your own life, when you go into a room, just think, well, let's see what I can do.

Many times, I think to myself, "I don't know what I'm going to do here. It's just such a hard room. How am I going do it? There's nothing to work with." Then I get stuck in, start moving stuff around, and suddenly everything falls together by itself. Sometimes this is how we need to look at life and our cocoons or potential, without knowing the answers. We just need to make the first move. It's almost like the river runs the other way, and then you say, "I never would have thought of that."

7 Reasons Why You Need Time Behind a Wall

1) Power to claim your Big Ass Hair Do

2) Know who you are and what you want

3) Selfish rules!

4) Gives you energy and enthusiasm to embrace the challenges of life

5) The power to ask for what you want

6) Creates boundaries - a must for survival

7) Alone time makes you confident by connecting to your Source

SELFISH ACTION

Buy a pretty book to hold your Self-ISH Rules and start writing them down.

Start dreaming about your chair or your chaise. What will you be sitting on when you are honing your Big Ass Hairtude? Test chairs at some local stores. Think about how you feel when you are sitting down. Do you enjoy putting your feet up? Do you want an ottoman? How wide should the chair be in order for you to be comfortable? Can you put your feet on the floor and do you want? Start looking at garage sales or consignment stores, or head out to Ikea, Room and Board, or Pottery Barn, or look for a higher end furniture store in your neighborhood or your nearest big city center. Do have a budget, and don't let lack of money stop you from finding that perfect seat. A chair or a chaise must feel comfortable and support you. Can you write in the chair? Does the chaise support your back? How big is your space, and can you get a big ass chair through the door? Color is important, too. Do you want your favorite color? Or do you prefer neutrals with a splash of color in the rug? Maybe you have a chair in your house or a color you are not crazy about. Don't worry—by the time you pull your room together, you will love how it looks. Think comfort, practicality, personal use, and big picture. Your room is becoming real; it all starts with a goal.

CHAPTER THREE

Surround Yourself

"ARRANGE WHATEVER PIECES COME YOUR WAY."
— *Virginia Woolf*

We've covered Selfish Space and why it is essential to pay yourself first—to take time to know yourself, set boundaries, and claim your Big Ass Hair Do. Now we move into the room. The pieces that come your way in life or in furniture are yours for the taking. Life can happen to you, while you sit around bemoaning what isn't, or you can grab on to what there is and fashion a place that supports you.

Surroundings. The word holds so much power. You are where and how you live. If you are surrounded by clutter, you feel trapped, unable to breathe. If you live in darkness, your soul longs for light. Even if you don't notice light or are color blind, you have to have a place to work. The most pedestrian of analysts agree that to be productive, people need an environment that facilitates productivity.

Claiming your space is the first step to Spiritual Renewal. Stop waiting for a better day or someday. There is no better moment than the present. Get out of your pain and into your claim. Stake your hold.

You might look at decorating magazines, pictures, or movies of people's wonderful environments and how they live and long for that. What you are longing for is not that person's home, but the connection that the space evokes within you.

A lot of people think design or decorating a space is a frivolous thing. I firmly believe that the way a room is arranged has a profound effect on how you feel in that room. Design is a huge part of our lives. It influences how you deal with life. When beauty and calm surround you, you feel in control, nurtured. That's why people are drawn to gardens and art. Being in the presence of beauty stirs up a blissful connection.

Design gives you power. When you create an environment that you enjoy, it speaks spiritually, physically, and energetically to your passion and to your gut.

Design is a tool. Surround yourself with ugliness, and you will feel bad. Great spaces frame your life. Why deny yourself the right to be in a space that delights you?

Successful people don't typically live in dumps. Fabulous surroundings make you feel confident and comfortable when inviting anyone to your home. I guarantee that when you dream of the spaces you want to live in, you are not imagining a dark space with a lumpy sofa pushed up against a wall.

Live the lifestyle you want and feel good about it.

Are you visual or kinetic? Do you need texture or light or color around you? How do you respond to your environment?

An artist cannot paint without light. We are all artists in our own way. We are creative creatures. We can hardly think in a space that is full of other people and other things. Everything around us is energy and has weight. Everything takes up space. When we walk into a room that we love, we feel light and happy. This gives us confidence and poise to do anything. That is how much our physical environment influences our every waking moment. Why do people love to go to luxurious hotels? To feel indulged, special, important. That is also why spas are decorated as plush sanctuaries.

Use Design Intention

I have witnessed many personal transformations take place when rooms were created with design intention. That's what I do for a living. I have seen people moved to tears of joy when their room is arranged right.

My client, Patty, had a house full of items she had inherited, for some time, she could not let go of them. When she called me, she was ready. Her life felt stagnant, and she needed a change. Patty wanted her stuff, and she wanted her home to feel pulled together. We moved her rooms around, stored a couple things in the garage, hung art, and rearranged accessories. She came home while we were still pulling things together and started putting some of her accessories back. I spent some time helping her adjust to having change. For many people, this process can be very emotional. Once they get over the shock, they are thrilled at the incredible energy the change brings.

Patty told me, "It looks great. I added a tiny bit more clutter, but immediately recognized that the elegance was dissipated and took it away (mostly!!)."

That was huge! She had a dramatic shift from the new energy in her home. In one night, she was able to let go of that need to have every single item visible.

Your space, particularly your Chic Cocoon, is yours. Own it. Claim it. Let it reflect you on your deepest level.

People's lives change dramatically once they change their spaces because they're open to new things. The new space clears up negative holding patterns.

Another client had a room she never used. We added color and moved around her furniture. She told me that so many incredible things had happened since we change the room. She had a place to entertain and feel confident, and all kinds of shifts started happening.

Many clients have revealed how much new energy and flow has happened from the physical movement. Suddenly, they are motivated to move forward in positive ways.

Take a few moments to explore how you feel about the room you are in now. Look around. What do your instincts tell you about the space you are in?

Stop making excuses about someday—there is no need to wait to act.

Remember what Woolf said about arranging whatever comes your way.

Sometimes when we are stuck, we don't even know it.

Do you feel like you need a change? Can you say yes to any of these statements?

Something feels wrong in the space.

I can't work or relax.

I have no motivation.

It feels too crowded.

I can't relate to the space.

I feel like going out and buying a new _____.

I am ashamed to invite anyone over.

Hence the thought that someday, one day, I'm going to get new curtains, or I'm going to break through that wall, or do whatever it is that you think will flip the switch on your room.

Here is a secret that will save you money and anguish:

You don't need to wait for someday, one day, because it's really about space—how you use space.

You can have a new room, in less than a day, without buying anything new. Make a commitment to get your room working for you. Begin with one small shift.

It's not what you have, but where it is placed and how it's put together that allows a room to breathe.

Great rooms are about bones and pizzazz. Personality is not connected to dollars. It comes from confidence and knowing what you like, just like pulling an outfit of clothing together.

It is possible to make changes on your own. You may have a very good eye.

Regardless, there's no harm in trying to change the room around.

The only thing you can lose is some time.

You are worth the investment. Pay yourself first. Your life cannot change unless you create the shift, by engaging in moving the pieces.

It is like playing real life monopoly. You get to choose what room you want to land on and how it feels.

Pulling a room together is about shape, volume, and relationship,

If you don't know where to start, do some research. Check out my blog, www.chiccocoon.com. There are many wonderful design blogs out there, to tempt you.

Check out my favorite on my website.

Don't think you need to slavishly copy what you see. Take your time and feel out what appeals to you. If your room feels boring, bring in color. Start with a pillow or a bowl of flowers.

Examine magazines, both online and hardcopies. Check out http://www.ruemag.com or http://dabblemag.com. Look at rooms you like, and get a feel for who you are. Follow a designer online that appeals to you. When you walk into a room that feels good, take note of what it is about that room that is calling your name.

Pay attention to art, and to colors. The appeal is often in the details.

Colors do look different in different rooms and different light, so test a color before painting. Paint a large sample board and move it around the room at different times of the day. Always check the color against a white background, so that the background color does not influence what you are looking at. Bring in color with accessories. It is amazing what accessories can do to change up a room. A favorite shawl or brightly colored art can quickly kick a boring room into high gear. Shop through your home or the thrift store, or try some online or local stores. Check out my website for suggestions.

Hire an expert if you need help. When you are ill, you visit a doctor. Think of your designer/decorator as a guide for healthy living.

It is worth the investment. This process is about recognizing you have a need, and if you don't know how to fix your own space, hire it out.

When I need help with something that I know nothing about, I don't do it myself, if I can help it. I hire someone.

Maybe the size of the task has put you into overwhelm. Take baby steps. Give yourself a goal that is doable. Make it a small stretch so you can feel good about your accomplishments. Set aside a fixed amount of time to go through ornaments you no longer need, start with one cabinet, one drawer, or one tabletop. And deal with everything once. If you love it, keep it. Put anything else in a pile or box with a finite time to decide, or toss it in the thrift store pile. Move the stuff into your car, ready for unloading at the thrift store. Get yourself an accountability partner, a friend who also needs to create her space. Take turns helping each other. Keep your goal in mind – to give you room to breathe. If you struggle with clutter or making a decision, get a book or find someone to help you.

You can quickly get on with doing what you are good at when you hire an expert, while reaping the benefit of room that makes your heart sing.

Be inspired!

This is your cloak against fear, against too much sorrow. When you are in a space that caresses you, how long can you indulge in a pity party? Use your environment as a shield and a comfort, to protect and cherish you. You will connect faster to your Inner Spirit when you are in your space.

In chapter 10, "Optimize Your Environment," of Marcia Conner's book, *Learn More Now*, she talks about how much the space you are in affects how you focus in it. (See www.marciaconner.com/learnmorenow/index.) Creating the right space includes obvious elements like seating and lighting, as well as sounds and nature. Inspirational items in the form of beauty and grace enhance your learning. Interestingly enough, snacking on the right foods can also increase your effectiveness. Making the right choices gives us a room to glow in.

Help yourself connect by maximizing your perfect spot. This is not your G-spot; it's your S-spot. That is right, your Sexy Selfish you. Take her out of her box where you have been hiding her and let her stretch her legs.

If you want to leap instead of crawl, or soar to meet your potential, you need to give your Inner Delicious self a voice and seat.

Having your own space is a shrine to yourself. Your cocoon is your place to wrap yourself up and be yourself every day. Sometimes, you may feel happy and joyful and feel like dancing. Some days, you may feel blue and miserable, and you want to wallow in that, and all that is fine. Having an escape room is a delicious secret.

After I rearranged her room, Darcie Newton told me, "You can change the energy so remarkably by just changing things around with furniture, pictures, and art objects. It's not just aesthetically more pleasing to the eye, the energy in the room changes. It changes how you feel about being in that room. It's amazing." Honestly, no matter how many times I have done this, I am astonished every time how incredible it really is. This process works.

Claiming Your Space

When we think about the word space, or a place we can go, we have to think so much larger than just four walls. There are so many spaces out there. The idea is not so much the space, but that it's the movement. It's moving yourself mentally and physically out of where you are. If you love gardening, it's wonderful to go into the garden and create a spot. If you don't have a garden, then you can certainly go into a public space or maybe a friend has a garden you can use. The importance is the time alone, so in inclement weather, you can go to a coffee shop, a museum, or a place where you've been longing to go. If you love to explore antiques, then go find an antique store and wander around. Treat yourself to a fabulous tea at a teashop or have a glass of wine. Visit the ocean or hit a library or a bookstore. There's choices galore, just find something that connects with you. If you're in a home that's a mess or you hate being in there, that's not a good place to hide out or to escape.

Having your own space is critical; it's all part of honoring and allowing yourself time to just be. I know that for practical reasons you may not have that spare room in your life right now. But don't give up. Consider your options.

Melanie told me, "I've been thinking about my own space. I don't have my own space in my house, and I'm figuring out where I'm going to do it because this is critical."

If you are like Melanie, and you want, need, and are looking for a space, here is a list to get you started:

7 Possibilities for Considering as Le Chic Cocoon

What size space do you need? What kind of space can you spare?

Sometimes we don't have control over our entire home, or our whole life, but we can fashion a space to escape to. Many times, we may have to wait to have the perfect spot, but to start, any space will do. Let your imagination and your will come to your aid. Trust your instincts and know what feels right. Compromise may be needed for the physical space, but no compromise is allowed for time in your space. Remember to focus on your goal—a space that supports your escape.

1) Creativity corner

If you don't have a room with walls, a door, and a key, you can certainly use a comfy chair in a corner as your space. The chair, a good light, and a table to hold your books, magazines, and Diva Accoutrement is big enough to begin your transformation.

Consider the landing space, a wall of the underused dining room or tucked away corner of the family room, shuttered with a screen when you are in session. You could also use a four-poster bed with hangings that hide and cover, or a curtained alcove, a window seat, or an empty closet you can convert.

2) Double up

Your bedroom can double up as your retreat, providing you have a space with a pleasing view and it is completely yours.

Your office or den can do double duty as your retreat, providing you have room to connect without distraction.

3) Bathroom

Many women find succor behind closed bathroom doors. Make yours a sybaritic paradise with bubble bath, thick fluffy towels, some candles, and even a bit of bubbly in the form of apple cider or champagne. Spoil yourself by lounging in the tub or on a cozy chair. As a woman who has had very little selfish space, one of my favorite choices was the bathroom. It is a great place to escape. Even if you share the bathroom, as long as there is a lock on the door, you have an ideal getaway. Invest some time and a little money to make your bathroom appealing. Spruce it up, paint the walls if you can.

4) An unused bedroom

Turn that unused bedroom or hardly used guest room into an away-from-it-all hideaway. If you are drawn to the idea of an island getaway, you can even post or hang a view of the ocean, add some palms, a wind machine, a coconut candle, and some tropical drinks with umbrellas in them. This is your dream room—create it in bold strokes to reflect your perfect escape.

5) A patio under a big tree, a secret tent, a folly in the garden or a cocoon hammock

Nature can be the most lush and giving space to engage your Inner Spirit. Let the sprite come out to play while you ponder the meaning of life in an outdoor room. Fill it up with greenery or flowering shade and sun plants, and some inspiring pieces, like a gazing ball, a trickling fountain, and some candles for night time star gazing and belly button contemplation.

6) Convert a partial garage, the attic, or the basement.

A coat of paint, a plush rug, and a sweet chandelier above your chaise, near a window. Paste an image on one big wall with a view or wash the walls with up-lights. You will be hard put to keep the family out of your secret room, but stand or sit strong.

7) The ultimate Chic Cocoon

A hideout that is all out is a room with a lock and key that has a view, natural light, and perhaps even an attached patio. It's big enough to have room to do it all—a turret room a studio or loft—whatever your dream space is.

EXERCISE:

Create a dream board of your perfect Chic Cocoon.

Gather some magazines, a board, glue and a pair of scissors and let your instincts take over. Don't over think or analyze, no matter how farfetched your room may appear. Just get into the Cocoonista groove and create— pull out cozy room photos, scenery words—whatever draws you. Set the timer and focus on creating your Selfish Space—with room for one only. This is your Sanctuary—there are no limitations and no compromises!

Put the board up or photograph it with your cell phone – make sure it's somewhere you can connect to and see it anytime you feel stressed, overwhelmed, sad, or happy. Keep the dream alive.

Personally, I am delighted to trail down a lane of exploration and discovery in pursuit of my Cocoon of Chic Deliciousness.

7 Elements to Inspire Us into Our Selfish Space

Once we have the ideal space, what do we put in it? Here is a list of my top seven items.

1. Space—a feeling of openness around one. High ceilings, a room with a view, uncluttered air—so there is room to dream.

2. Light—a delicious view, a sexy chandelier, light to work by.

3. Quiet—when there is noise around us (unless we are really in tune with ourselves or very good at sinking into our own subliminal space), we need quiet. According to psychologist Dr. Mary W. Meagher's Texas A&M University Study, women actually get stressed faster than men in noisy environments, (see this study at www.fi.edu/learn/brain/stress).

4. Color is a huge transformer. There is so much healing and happiness in color. And each of us has our own power colors. We are also drawn to certain colors when we are seeking the benefits those colors give us. Your instincts are so valuable in determining what colors to pick, whether it's on the walls or in a pillow or rug. Don't be put off if you

can't paint because you're in a rental or some other reason.

If you want to make a color disappear, bring in the opposite color to balance it. Rooms change with color. Color can come in so many guises. Consider nature's bounty, like a rock, to handmade art, like a piece of pottery. Choose from a simple colorful bunch of flowers to a pile of books, or a rare piece of art to wake up a room. There are so many avenues you can explore to discover your missing piece of color.

5. Inspiration—every creative corner needs something to inspire your inner dreamer. Maybe it is a piece of art that that explodes with excitement. Perhaps it's a bowl of marble eggs, a gift from a loved one, an incredible view, or some soul-soaring music. Inspiration is derived from an emotion that connects and delights your inner you.

6. Activity—the key to being in creative consciousness is doing something that unlocks the key. Like journal writing, looking at colors or travel magazines, dancing, banging the drum, or meditating. Whatever it is, make sure that you have it at hand in your secret dream room. Perhaps you need a few different modalities to fit your mood of the moment.

7. Time - perhaps the most important of all is to block out the appointment, make this a daily ritual. Even ten minutes a day of mindless drawing or listening to music that is just for you can change your mood. Lighten your load and strengthen you. The creative outpouring that flourishes in your unfettered mind might astonish you.

Describe your perfect hideaway:

Name Your Room:

Whatever the size, make the room part of your life by giving her a name, creating a personality. This is the space that will shelter and cherish your inner She—your sexy, sensual Divine Diva. Give her the love, the softness, and the welcome she delights in and craves.

How do you know if your space works for you? When you feel blissful about being in your personal space that feels like it reflects you. Usually, my clients walk around, touching all their stuff after a room makeover. Their old stuff is reignited. The room becomes a sanctuary to entertain and to enjoy the essence of their lives. The designer aesthetic brings a sexy comfortable look into the home.

An artist friend, Corinne Friedman, www.artfulshoes.com, whose home is filled with personal pieces, tells me her friends always that say that her space is an expression of who she is. What can be more delicious and grounding than that?

Working Space

"You are a product of your environment. So choose the environment that will best develop you toward your objective. Analyze your life in terms of its environment. Are the things around you helping you toward success - or are they holding you back?"

---W. CLEMENT STONE

You may be fortunate enough to have a space to work in and a space to dream in—two separate spaces. Sometimes we have to share two roles in one room—just like we have shared two women in one body—our polite outer shell and our inner Diva. Now that you are beginning to get closer to your inner woman, you no longer have to share. You have merged. Let the real you show up, and be present in your life. Hiding will never get you want you want. You can definitely share a working, resting space if you set it up that way. Keep your work clutter under control so you can shut the door on it. Create a corner that is your Chic Cocoon with an inspirational view. Add some plants or personal items, a favorite rug. A workspace is more inviting when it's decorative and functional.

It should reflect you because studies show that your work environment makes a huge difference in how well you perform. Surrounding yourself with things that inspire you is an essential part of working. Motivation comes easily when you have a fabulous view or a vase of flowers that delight you. Your energy level increases, and your mental outlook and thought process shifts into high gear in a supportive environment. It's no coincidence that wealthy people have beautiful offices. The great view is a nod to your importance and success. It's hard to feel empowered in the dark.

Having personal beloved pieces around you are key, even if you're in a place that is out of your control. You can have a wall poster with a glorious view, a piece of art, or a fabulous container filled with flowers that you can gaze at. It is a reminder, a talisman.

Some women are going to tell me that they have always worked in a less than ideal environment, and it's perfectly fine—they have always been successful.

My response? Why not invest in yourself and make it even better? How much more successful could you be in a space that energizes you? After all, you might as well enjoy where you spend most of your life. You are worth it.

What are the benefits of a room of your own?

Power over your own space gives you incredible courage, incentive, and the ability to see your potential. It is a space to be you.

Surround yourself not just with things you love – whether new or old, found or given—but also with people you love. Be in control in your space. Create the boundaries for how people treat you and for who you let into your space.

Be aware of how much energy it takes from you. Everything light and bright has an energy that is irresistible. And the opposite is true of the heavy energy of the dark. It is so easy to get sucked into other people's stories, their sorrow, and their pain.

Acknowledge their story, but don't try to fix it, or fix them. Breathe out and let go of their baggage.

We cannot live for other people. We need to be true to ourselves so that we can help those that depend on us. We are allowed to make the rules. We are the Rulers in our world.

You cannot change or control anyone. You can only change yourself, your attitude, your perspective.

The best way to do this effectively is through your surroundings. What are you drawn to? Is there a color you love?

A book, or a piece of art, or an inspirational saying that captures your essence? Surround yourself with color, texture, and materials that speak to you.

SELFISH ACTION

Take a long bubble bath, with the door locked. Bring in a glass of bubbly, light some candles, and visualize your ideal Chic Cocoon. See yourself in your space, doing what you love.

If you want to add a little dazzle to your bathroom, walk in and give it a good look.

Are the tiles in good shape? Do the walls or the cabinets need paint? Painting cabinets and changing knobs, replacing the light fixture or taps can be impact items that won't break the bank if you shop wisely. Check out hardware stores, Ikea, and Restoration Hardware.

Can you live with the color and just add accessories?

Buy some new towels. TJ Max, Pottery Barn, and Horchow all have different styles and prices. Pick a color that compliments the tile. If you are not sure, check out a color wheel to learn how colors relate. Have some fun mixing stripes and dots or florals with plain towels if the tile is a basic color, or has an accent color you can use. If you stick to a couple of colors that you pick up from what is fixed (things you can't change without spending big money), you can make a big impact. There are a lot of fun shower curtains at Target, or make your own and put a liner underneath. Bring in a sexy container to hold soaps and assorted items. Splurge on a luxury bath product. Change the mirror or put your own frame around it from the hardware store or check out Mirror Mount. Bring in artwork that matches your color scheme and is resistant to dampness and moisture. A plant, some candles, and a little chair or ottoman, if you have room, can add so much warmth. This is your room, so treat it with love and remember restraint. Don't go overboard and buy everything and fill every corner. Just decorate enough.

CHAPTER FOUR

Dream to Do

"IT IS IN OUR IDLENESS, IN OUR DREAMS, THAT THE
SUBMERGED TRUTH SOMETIMES MAKES ITS WAY TO THE
SURFACE."

— *Virginia Woolf*

In the previous chapter, we talked about getting started finding your personal Cocoon space. Once you have the space, or you acknowledge the need for one, you can begin to get creative.

There are a million ways to be creative. And you should feel free to be "idle" in any way you choose. This is your time. You can lie down in long grass, smell the earth, and look at the sky. You can walk along the shore and breathe in salty air, make sand angels, or roll down the hill. Have your nails done. Or perhaps you can escape to a bookstore to pore over dusty tomes, sit in a sidewalk café, drinking a long cool drink or a glass of wine, enjoying the freedom of an empty mind. Perhaps page through glossy magazines and tear out pictures to create your own vision board—whatever activity lets your mind roam free. Use your time doing something that allows you to truly let go, daydream, and hum. Feel totally free. This is your time. No one can interrupt you, call you, or break the spell. The only rule is that it is your rule. This is your opportunity to suspend time and shoulds, to clear the decks and honor yourself. If you cannot think of what to do to be creative, do nothing. When was the last time you scheduled yourself a "do nothing day," when you were totally free?

Jot down the last time 3 times you gave yourself a day off.

1. _____

2. _____

3. _____

If you had a free day right now, what would you do?

Everyone is capable of being creative, especially you! Shut your ears to the naysayers and jump in. Life is derived from creativity. We fashion our worlds, our very existence, on creative elements.

Get creative, let down your guard, and for those moments, let your inner child, the one you abandoned, come out and play.

Put yourself in a space that awakens your body.

Tina Seelig is Executive Director for the Stanford Technology Ventures Program (STVP), the entrepreneurship center at Stanford University's School of Engineering. She is also the author of *What I Wish I Knew When I Was Twenty: On Making Your Place in the World,* in which she shares nine ways to unlock your creativity quotient. Check them out at http://havefundogood.blogspot.com/2011/02/tina-seeligs-9-ways-to-unlock-your.html.

One of my favorites is Observation: Pay attention. The answers you're looking for may be right in front of you.

She also talks about space—how your environment helps or hampers your creativity. Creativity and function are enhanced with the right surroundings. You have to feel like you can move if you need to. I find my creative mind is in the flow when I engage my body.

Dance, squish your toes in mud, pick up a pencil and paper, or play music. With no agenda in mind, make that brain candy swirl.

Opening up the creativity door is essential, so give yourself time.

Refer to Chapter 3 for 7 Elements to inspire us into our Selfish Space.

Suspend Judgment.

You don't know what you can do till you do it. So get your inner critic to shut up.

Conscious connections happen when you're completely wrapped up and doing something you love.

It's like this happiness that spreads inside ourselves in our brains, and it fires off neurons that we don't even know about. So while we're drifting off into this creative world, we're actually allowing our senses and our intuition to bubble away and light up. It gives us a different point of view. Try mind mapping to unlock your creativity. There are many online tools or methods you can engage with.

Connect to your inner Child - find your unique creative angle.

We all have a part of us that is playful and touches into what's essential to us in a happy way. Perhaps puzzling over something, or diving into the depths of a subject is what turns you on. We all have our creative essence, so it doesn't matter whether you hated drawing at school. You don't have draw now to be creative. You can do whatever it is that you love doing, no matter what it is, no matter your judgment. It's okay to be in that space and indulge that part of you. It does release stress because we build up so much pressure on ourselves when we fail to smell the roses, taking time to just enjoy the magic. Take yourself back to when you were a kid and relive a moment that made you ecstatically happy. When you laugh or play with your dog, that's being creative. You're allowing yourself to be a child, just enjoying the moment. You release the part of yourself or pressure on your brain that's pushing you down and stopping you from looking at life from a happy perspective. When you get all stressed out, everything becomes a problem. It's much easier to deal with life when you see it as a happy thing.

Change your point of view.

Take a problem and turn it around. Remove the emotion around it. When I go into a home to rearrange a room, that is creative. It's using my brain and body together. That is so delicious, I love it. The best part is I don't feel any emotion to any objects in the room. So it becomes a puzzle that I am excited to unlock. Sometimes you walk into a room and you think that things need to be in a certain place.

Ask yourself why? Why can't I change something that has always been done a certain way?

Maybe moving furniture holds no joy for you; perhaps you would rather be in the kitchen experimenting with a new recipe, or reading something that you totally disagree with. Can you suspend judgment long enough to open your mind? Work on a brainteaser or sing.

Move your body.

Awaken your kinetic self. Open up your senses. Get out of your head. Move, dance, sing, and swing. Do yoga. I always find such energy and joy when I focus on my body and let it play. It feels terrific to have my body and mind as one—like a fine-tuned musical instrument.

Create your own self-portrait.

Who are you? Draw it, write it, sing it, and make a video or collage of you. Try creating a life-size portrait. Really get to the meat of you. You might surprise yourself.

Take a step into your past.

"The biggest adventure you can ever take is to live the life of your dreams."

---OPRAH WINFREY, *O MAGAZINE*

Be a Dreamer

Ironic, that when I look back to my past, the biggest sin was to be labeled a dreamer. *Jennifer daydreams in class.* Underlined! Why that is a fault and not a reason to celebrate? When we are growing up, society is constantly trying to squeeze us all into tiny round holes. It feels like we spend the first 10 years of our lives walking barefoot, letting insects crawl on our arms, standing in the sunlight aglow with life, and suddenly someone throws the switch. We are in darkness, flailing about, trying to make sense of what happened. How did the light go out? When? Fast forward 30 years, and we are choking in the dust, scarcely aware of what we once dreamed. That is why it is essential to follow Virginia Wolfe's advice and give ourselves permission to do nothing. Daydreaming is a gift; it's a positive affirmation of who we are. It makes us believe in ourselves.

Darcie Newton told me she never has a problem going to sleep because, "I put my head down, and I start thinking about that brain candy (that is what I call it), and before I know it, I'm asleep. It's always wonderful thoughts." It's so delicious, relaxing your brain with yummy candy explosions, butterflies floating inside your head.

What's your favorite daydream?

I hope it's one where you are playing the heroine of your life, not being rescued by a knight in shining armor. Too many times, women are portrayed as creatures too weak to even save themselves from their miserable lives. The truth is we are the only ones that can save ourselves. You don't need a white charger or a man in any kind of suit. You just need a room of your own, with your permission to dream.

Without daydreams, we cannot create big visions. You think about something, letting your mind wander, then suddenly, BAM you get this amazing idea. That's what happens every day. You're daydreaming about something you heard and suddenly, you get the answer to a problem you've been thinking about. Dreams enable us to imagine a result and work toward it in tiny increments. After all, what are goals but the extension of a dream? I believe human beings are propelled by daydreams.

It is believed by some that the words "I know that" are in the dangerous words category. According to Elizabeth Donati, these three words cause mental shutdown. We close our minds when we say the words. Typically, when we say those words, we are responding to someone who is showing or telling us something. Maybe we don't want to hear it. Whatever the reason, the mind shuts down to any new information. Elizabeth Donati, The Ultimate Allowance, ultimateallowancebook.com/blog/?p=20 .

Think about it. Are you saying "I know that" to more than you should—shutting down your inner voice, your creative woman? Are you open to hearing new ideas about yourself, shifting your opinion, suspending judgment, and letting your playful side come out?

Let go of the need for the good opinion of others.

> *"Literature is strewn with the wreckage of men who have minded beyond reason the opinions of others."*
>
> ---VIRGINIA WOOLF

Definition of *OPINION*
www.merriam-webster.com/dictionary/opinion

1

a: a view, judgment, or appraisal formed in the mind about a particular matter

b: approval, esteem

2

a: belief stronger than impression and less strong than positive knowledge *b* : a generally held view

Trust your own instincts. Seeking approval or the good opinion of our peers, our parents, or anyone is a waste of energy. What if we want to do what we love and they don't approve? Then we stop ourselves from following our dreams. Do you want to live someone else's life or your own? We expend an extraordinary effort stressing about other opinions. Breathe out and let go. Everyone has an opinion. Decide for yourself. Form your own opinion. Let others be free to hold their opinions. Every time I have trusted my instincts and disregarded the generally held view, I have been successful.

Learning from or having an expert provide guidance and constructive criticism is a good thing. I am addressing judgment and family and peer pressure in this section.

I was at an event, and a woman tried to swallow a sneeze and she thought it sounded like a snicker while somebody was speaking. She was mortified, convinced she had insulted this woman, and that everybody knew it. That night, she couldn't sleep because she was so upset, and she made herself ill. I said to her, "What would have happened if you hadn't swallowed your sneeze?" She experienced a total AHA moment, realizing that she had suffered agony over assumption and opinion. If you need to sneeze, sneeze. The world will survive.

Stop assuming anything—you don't know how creative you are until you take a risk.

Being motivated or stopped by assumptions is so dangerous because assumptions have no basis in reality. Being a slave to assumptions or the opinion of others is serious dream-crushing material. We need our Big Ass Dreams so we can embrace our Big Ass Hair Do's.

"Well, what if I do it anyway?"

There is something so sexy, so appealing, about people who are independent of others. That is why girls are drawn to the bad boy at school—he represents what we long for—the fearlessness to thumb our noses at society.

If you want to find your creative depth, then you must be willing to look like a fool.

Yes, you do have to plan and work for it, but it is within your reach.

Remember your Self-Hood List in Chapter 2. Check it to see if what you want breaks your rules. If not, then go for it, baby!

Dredge up a dream.

Rediscover a childhood dream that you gave up because you were afraid. Pull it out and see if you can make it happen, no matter how simple or silly. What did you long to do? Sometimes journaling can clue you in to your past.

Keep the light within burning.

I come from a country that is full of people that are desperately poor. Yet every time I go home, I am astonished at the creativity that is fashioned from other people's discards. Pieces of wire, coat hangers, and plastic bags, baskets made from grass. My mouth hangs open with the beauty of the creations. Stop telling yourself you can't. Find the little light within that is still burning and flame it higher. You don't need to be famous, or draw like Rembrandt—you need to flame the passion for you. No matter how dark it feels, know you are not alone. You can do it. It may take time, habit and structure, but the light, the joy, is within your reach.

*"Women need a space to be creative—
creativity thrives in solitude. "*

---SUSAN ARIEL RAINBOW KENNEDY
(SUCCULENT WILD WOMAN)

Just as we dress ourselves to look good, to make us feel aglow, to be confident, as we paint a picture of who we are in dress, we must do the same in our home. We often say things like "our home is our temple." Is your home a temple to your inner woman? Do you feel a burst of joy as you enter? Are you energized and electrified when you get home? Do you feel cozy and warm, like you are in a cocoon, with a hammock of love, a nest to rest, reflect and rejuvenate? Make that part of your creative journey. Find your inner woman and let her shine in her temple.

Let go of the opinions of others.

Take time to dream.

Suspend judgment.

Don't assume. Ask.

Move your body.

Change your point of view.

Get creative.

SELFISH ACTION

Dance under the stars alone and enjoy the mind-body connection.

Create your outdoor room. Finding garden furniture can be easy. Look for garage sales and moving sales. Lots of stores have sales before the summer is over. Try sprucing up what you have. Pick inspiration from something in your garden or use your favorite color again. Spray paint or staining works wonders. Create a sitting area. Use brick, stone, ground cover, or pebbles. Throw down an outdoor rug. A fountain always adds a lovely sound. Group a bunch of pots together, painting them the same color, or painting stripes, spots or whatever you want. Bring the kids out to help you. Outdoor lighting makes it magic. String up some lights, set out some candles in a hurricane or lantern. Pile up a couple of rugs to cozy up in. Invest in some outdoor glasses and plates.

CHAPTER FIVE

Nourish to Flourish

"ONE CANNOT THINK WELL, LOVE WELL, SLEEP WELL,
IF ONE HAS NOT DINED WELL."
— *Virginia Woolf, A Room of One's Own*

This quote gets to the root of it all. Life is a banquet, one that not many women have been trained to dine well on. Yet we cannot honor our selves, we cannot grow or absorb what we need to, if we cannot sit at the grand table of life. If we deny ourselves the big banquet, we settle for the scraps. Apologizing, simpering, and hiding behind smallness will not give us a life that is nourished, balanced, and delicious.

We have the ability to do so much to claim our power. Lift our eyes off the lowly ground and connect with the big world—meet meet life, with our eyes open. Be aware, without pretending, hiding, or ducking in the shadow of the wall.

Life is an equalizer. If you believe you deserve the goodness, the sauces that have been reduced to the essence of all the elements that turn an ordinary meal into a queenly feast, then you need to show up to the table with gusto. You need to be willing to set boundaries. Plunge your dagger into the table, bang your fork! Know your enemy and win her respect. Be fearless. You will dine well, and when you dine well, you life will open to the aromas, tastes, and sensuality of a table groaning with abundance.

Often, it takes a transition in our lives to realize how much time has been spent living life as a reflection—through others, being there in person, but not in spirit—and not taking care of your inner core, not being true to yourself.

Chop hopeless off at less.

A good look can uncover gifts you can't see.

Rebecca has taken care of people her whole life. She was disappointed in her husband, feeling hopeless, and using anti-depression medication to keep smiling at the world. She admitted she was staying in a stagnant place out of fear. I think hope is the first step to conquer fear. Rebecca felt hopeless, convinced she had no skills to leverage. She needed to reframe the problem. What skill and knowledge do you have that can be used to create what you want? Use what you know, just look at "what" in a new way. Try mind mapping, or word association, gather a group of trusted women to guide and inspire you.

Make a list with four columns:

1) Experience, including life skills
2) Free association possibilities
3) What you enjoy
4) What you don't enjoy

Play around with the information without over thinking it. Open your mind.

An acquaintance is in a two-career marriage. Overwhelmed with trying to have it all and do it all, she must be at work at 7 am because her type of work demands it. This leads to so much stress and resentment in the family triangle. Spending time with kids becomes another chore we argue about with our spouse. We don't change our lives by lamenting them or building resentment. Very little in life is not negotiable—we need to accept what we want and cut the strings. Take the medicine. Negotiate with the spouse to change his hours. Hire someone to be a loving substitute, or negotiate with the boss. We are connected to our lives. We need to speak our truth and take action to make it happen. Ask for what you want and let them know where you are willing to be flexible. Take the resentment and guilt out of the equation.

We make our rules.

Get out of that story you tell yourself. Wake up. Slap some water on your face or go take a cold shower. You are the author of your life. Start writing the script. Do you want to linger in victimhood, or are you ready to hit that baby in the rear?

Every successful, dynamic Cocoonista determines her life, builds in balance, connects to her core.

Brandy Mychals creator of the Character Code System™, told me:

"As a woman, I used to believe that you could have it all and that you had to do it all. Now I know that you need to prioritize the things you want that matter and collaboration is key. Doing it on your own is overrated! As far as having balance, I reached a certain level of peace when I realized the 'to-do' list was never done. And, that was just perfect. Measure your progress based on forward movement and not checked-off items. Having set 'off' hours and shortening my work day actually made me productive and more time for fun!"

If you are interested in changing your life and discovering who you are, you have to make the commitment to go inside into a Chic Cocoon and into yourself. It can't just be on the surface. You can't pay lip service to it because that won't work. If you want it, you have to do the work. You have to go through the pain of stripping down your soul and facing yourself and really believing. Coming to the point that you do love yourself and you can honestly look at yourself and say, "I love you," takes work. It takes a lot of inward reflection to be able to admit when you've done something wrong and to ask for forgiveness and to feel okay about it. It's okay to acknowledge that you made a mistake. It's okay to feel the pain and the process; it's like we're stretching into another space. It reminds me of the cartoon when the human body has to change into Spiderman, and there's this painful pulling and tearing, you can see the body is changing. I think this is part of what transformation is; diving deep is painful. It's hard, and sometimes we don't want to do it. We don't feel like doing it. We don't feel like showing up for ourselves and admitting that we do some awful things to people just because we don't want to deal with why we're doing it. We have to go to the core. If you want to stop something, you have to really get to the reason why you're doing it. That's the huge part about growth. It has to be real. Realize that all those steps you took, all those things that you thought were wrong steps, were actually leading to where you are now. You wouldn't be where you are if you didn't have those experiences. So it's all connected in the circle of life.

You can have it all, just not in the proportions you were told. That "all" we are talking about means all that you value. Only keep what resonates with you. The rest you need to negotiate, settle, let go of. We can't be all things to all people, that is why we need to know what we want first.

What is your true definition of success?

Mine is doing work that stretches my soul and mind. I love traveling, laughing, loving myself this moment, and all those in my life. I also love living well in body, soul, and physical space. There is no compromise on what is important to me. I am living by my rules, while respecting the rules of others without necessarily agreeing. I am being joyfully bountiful and bountifully joyful.

You cannot stand tall or be there for anyone in any real way for a lasting period of time if you ignore your core. There are many times when the transitions can be painful and full of fear, like a child going off to college, a divorce, or death. Events like these make us stop to question who we are and where are we going in our lives. Many times it takes a lifetime lived in someone else's shoes, being a dedicated employee, a wife, a mother, a daughter playing a role, but not being who we actually are. That is what often spirals into a crisis as our reason for those roles falls away. You are a successful, resourceful, opinionated woman who has no place to hide, no place to lick your wounds in peace, not even a broom cupboard where you can hunker down and cry or indulge your inner woman, or even drink a shitload of martinis. Watch soppy soaps, gobble up ice cream and chocolates. Perhaps put up an easel and paint or write that novel that is locked in your heart. Claim your Breathing Room.

Going through transitions is a huge part of realizing that we have to honor ourselves and give ourselves room and permission to live for us habitually. Whatever it is that's turning you on, you should be doing it for yourself.

Journal through your changes; you can jot down a note or write as much as you need to give clarity to your personal experiences.

"Your journal becomes the trusted friend you can talk to. It allows you to connect with yourself and learn who you are without critique or judgment."
--Judy Peebles, The Journaling Jenius™and creator of *The Knowledge Series – Your Key to Success*

Record your story, using whatever method works for you:

    Writing
    Talking – you can record this for later.
    Creating collages
    Drawing

"Another day honoring my commitment to myself, are you honoring your commitments to yourself and in turn honoring yourself? Would love to know because hell it's not an easy path sometimes, but my advice is pick one thing and master it and then add something else, overwhelm is a commitment killer! Step by step is the way"
--Shivie Cook www.thecookandbutler.com

Nourish Yourself

We need to think about ourself and our internal person, our heart and our head, and really fill them with stuff that we want to know because I think a lot of times, as women, we tend to just learn what is expedient. We open ourselves on a need to know basis—for example, how do we help the kids get better grades, or help them feel more confident--but we don't think about that in terms of ourselves. We need to open our spirits and minds up to learning new things, whatever they may be. It can be some crazy idea that's just off the wall. You wake up one morning and you think to yourself, "I'd love to learn how to do patchwork," or "I would be enchanted to grow an herb garden. I just love to understand why I always feel the way I do. Why do I keep going back into these patterns?"

Opening yourself up to the possibility that nourishment comes from experimenting. When you're having a nourishing meal, you choose items that are really tasty, full of vitamins, look appealing, and you enjoy it. That is how I want you to approach the idea of nourishing yourself. Take in tantalizing things that are full of good stuff you crave, so you can expand yourself, get taller. Improve your vision. You decide what appeals to you; there is no judgment on your interest. Variety is infectious.

Search for things you're interested in and become more interesting and rounded. Be soft in your strength, womanly.

Life is full of inspiration, but so many of us wear blinkers. We have tunnel vision. We're too busy trying to cross the road and focused on all the shoulds and a laundry list of things that need to get done. With the misconception that we can't have a good time, there can be no looking out there and seeing what's possible until we have done "our homework" and completed our chore list.

When you are looking out and you see something that just catches your eye, you walk toward it, grab it, and it expands you. Why can't we meander sometimes? Why can't we see our view from the other side of the road?

I was reading Judy Stone-Goldman's post, at http://www.thereflectivewriter.com, where she talks about someone sharing their perspective of Judy's puzzle. This was a completely new way of looking at the problem to Judy. Pondering this different perspective of her life, Judy went into a labyrinth that she often walks through, and this time she saw the labyrinth in a completely new light. Looking at our lives from a different door definitely opens up so many possibilities. Life can feel so dull and miserable when we're following the path that we think we have to take. Sometimes, it feels like we're shut down and that there's no light in the room, no hope. But just by being aware that we can enter our lives through the front door, like a guest, we can suddenly be in the light. This knowledge can brighten up your whole day, your very existence.

I don't think that it's the act of travel or getting somewhere and moving elsewhere that changes our soul or broadens our mind. It's going somewhere where we actually get to see familiar objects from a different point of view. We're amazed when we have been living a certain way so long and find people on the other side of the world have been living in a completely different way with those same objects. It opens up our minds to new possibilities. We can be anything and do anything—even though we're creatures of habit, we don't need to stay in those habits. We can experiment and take our time to think about who we are. We don't need to figure it out right now. We don't have to wake up tomorrow morning and know exactly where we're going. We just need to have a plan or an idea of a place we want to get to for today, or maybe next week, or perhaps in two years. If we start on that path, things will open up and we will find something new.

I took a workshop and realized that I had been looking down all the time when I walked. How interesting is that? It turns out that when you're looking down, like the caterpillar, you're keeping your vision in a very small space, so all you can see is a limited view. When you lift your eyes up to the horizon, suddenly you have this incredible view of what's out there in front of you. So when you're in a job you hate and you crouch around it, feeling so miserable that you close yourself off, you can't see what else is out there. There is an escape route; broaden your mind and change your point of view.

Don't most women feel fulfilled already?

I think that's an illusion. We tell ourselves we're fulfilled because we have everything that somebody else has decided that we need. We have children, a career, a home, and friends. But I think it's all linked somewhere inside. If we're not connected and grounded to ourselves, it can feel like something is missing. We're each so different in so many ways, but yet we have a cookie cutter life set out before us. We wake up and have all these expectations, just like a ten-step program of what we need to do. Yet for each of us, there's some niggling thought inside that's rejecting the sameness without a personal connection to our inner woman. As little kids hanging out with a bunch of friends, everyone was excited and fascinated about something completely different. When we grow up, we look at our lives and say, "I have a great house, and I have the perfect family—why aren't I happy?" What is the point? You do the stuff because you need to, and you love helping your family and having a great home around you. There is that inner you that's crying out for a break from the routine, needing something personal for which to strive. It doesn't have to be deep. You definitely want to have moments to smell the roses or get your nails done, go river rafting, or whatever your personal pull is in order to make you feel connected, whole , and to experience that life pulse.

Figure out what you truly want, not what you think you should want. Truly filling your life with what you want will give you that sense of fulfillment. It's a matter of choosing with deliberate action.

A lot of women define themselves by their family.

That's a problem. You're defining yourself by other people. It's great to enjoy what your family does and celebrate it' there's nothing more thrilling. But they are not who you are. Family maybe a large part of your life, but it is still not who you are as a person.

So, when your kids grow up and leave, if your husband decides to split, or if your life somehow changes, all these parameters alter, and then what do you have? If you don't know who you are, if you don't have something that belongs entirely to you, you fall apart.

A woman needs to separate herself from her family. Being part of a group is very important to a human being, but first you need to stand alone. You can't stand alone if you think of yourself as more than one person. When you are six people, how do you make a decision? How do you focus? How do you set boundaries? You can't have the answers until you separate yourself and be an individual. First, you stand as one, then you stand as a group, because then you each connect to the core of who you are and make decisions based on true desires. How exciting is that?

Seven Ideas to Awaken the Inner Woman

Growing and nourishment should all take place in your Chic Cocoon, in your personal exploration room. Real or imaginary, the room with a key will support and feed you.

Once you understand what's important to you, then it's becomes simple to make decisions because you have inner knowledge, which is essential for a fulfilled life. It gives you a sense of inner peace.

Do you ever ask, "What's the purpose of my life?" Self-discovery unlocks your creative self and opens up doors and windows to gifts.

1. Write: journal—get to the root of your own feelings—know thyself: really get to whatever you're feeling, or thinking, put that on paper. Get into the habit of doing a daily journal to express and connect to your deepest feelings. See your journal as somebody you're talking to, where you can reveal your private thoughts and begin to see patterns in your life. Check out Judy's blog, www.thereflectivewriter.com, for some wonderful prompts to get you in the mood or sign up for a journaling workshop with Judy Peebles at http://thejournalingjenius.com.

2. Ask: use spiritual cards or self-discovery books or tapes to listen to your inner Spirit. What are you neglecting? If you don't know, maybe a coach can help you or you can read a book about self-discovery. What are you missing in your life? What are you ignoring? For me, I discovered there have been many things I ignored or reacted to without thinking. Knowing what I wanted and how to get it was part of my discovery. Use this book as a discovery tool. Your strength becomes knowing your weaknesses so you can work on them.

3. Move, yoga or dance—you can use movement to change your life. Understand and connect with your body using a medium you enjoy. This really opens up your heart because we are physical beings, and in the world we live in right now, we forget how important the relationship is between body and mind. Without the body, we would be minds on a shelf, and we can't do anything if we're just the mind. The body and the mind are a team, and the mind can feel so much joy in the body's movement. Try dancing, running, or taking a walk. I always find my perspective changes when I'm moving because I feel energetic and receptive.

4. Plan: Magazines meander—create your vision board or life path- be actively creating the big you: plan out what

you want to do. Create a vision board, using magazines. Pull out the pictures and words that draw you. Dream about what you want and need out of your life while you're doing it. Just be free and believe there are no limitations. I also create boards on my computer, since I have access to many images. I download that where I can see it, or print it out to remind myself daily.

5. Sound: Sing, play, vibrate music or listen to music. Free up space in your mind—let your inner child in: Making sounds is very powerful for the body. We laugh, that's a sound that makes us happy. I laugh when I hear other people laugh. I love to laugh. It is joyful. Maybe you like to sing, act out a play, hum, or listen to bells. Free space in your mind and let go, listen to your heart. Stop thinking and be. Whatever sound you're creating, even if you sing off key, if it feels good, do it. I attended a sound workshop where we got to make the sounds of feelings in and outside our head. Human beings respond to the vibration of sound in a big way.

6. Contemplate: meditate, or daydream to connect with your spiritual self: go to a quiet place where you can think or just be. Sometimes just being, changing your space, going into a garden, a church, or a space that has spiritual meaning for you where you can be quiet is all it takes. Release extraneous thoughts in your head and just be in a moment of quiet contemplation.

7. Doodle, paint, garden, or knit: get creative so you can paint, garden, and do something that opens up your creative gates. Even if you don't know how to draw, just get some pencils and a piece of paper and start. Take finger paints and splatter them around or dig in the dirt, connecting with an activity that frees the mind. Your head is open, your heart is open, and you're letting thoughts and ideas come to you. Your inner critic is pre-occupied, which is essential for awakening your inner self and

creating conversations with yourself with no preset questions or answers.

Darcy: *"For me, gardening is the form of meditation, so when I'm out in the garden and I'm weeding, my mind is clear because I'm very focused on what I'm doing. I'm not thinking about what I'm having for dinner or what marketing I haven't done. I'm thinking, 'Okay, that's a weed, that's not a weed, that's a weed.' It's a very repetitive task, but it helps me. I find joy in beauty, so I feel very calm focused and centered. It's lovely."*

When we do an automatic, repetitive task that involves our mind and body, that we are focused on, it frees up that creative section in ourselves that we often suppress, our inner dreamer. That's why showering, putting on makeup, or driving bring forth nuggets. Our censor is pre-occupied with the task at hand. That is a meditative state that connects you to your Inner Spirit.

Most women are so busy, how do you find the time to do this?

Choice. It's up to us to decide, set boundaries, mark out a space, and make a conscious choice that we want change. Change comes through action. The first action is taking the time to figure out what it is that we want to change. Studies prove that by carving out the time in your day and marking the action in your calendar, more time opens. You feel wonderful because you've taken time for yourself in your Chic Cocoon and freed up space in your head. You've cleaned out the clutter—there's no more walking around all day with this big balloon weight above your head, thinking about your problems. You've thought about it, written about it (for example) and let it go; time is gained. Your life becomes more relaxed, you can live in the moment, and you feel exhilarated.

Learning new things takes time, be patient. A child doesn't learn to tie his shoes without taking time to learn. Why do you expect yourself to know new things without effort and time?

Skip multitasking. Be in the moment. Focus on the task at hand and let the other stuff go.

It is not how much you do, but how well you do what is important to you.

"We are not what we know but what we are willing to learn."

---MARY CATHERINE BATESON

SELFISH ACTION

Pick something you have been longing to learn, no matter how crazy or silly it feels, and just do it. Take the first step toward your independence. Maybe learn how to strip, paint, and reupholster that chair you need for your Chic Cocoon. It feels so good to do and discover things just for the sheer enjoyment of it. Go into the kitchen and make a recipe you have been dying to try, or take up horseback riding. Set at date to celebrate you.

CHAPTER SIX

Cocoon Chic

"BY HOOK OR BY CROOK, I HOPE THAT YOU WILL POSSESS
YOURSELVES OF MONEY ENOUGH TO TRAVEL AND TO IDLE,
TO CONTEMPLATE THE FUTURE OR THE PAST OF THE WORLD,
TO DREAM OVER BOOKS AND LOITER AT STREET CORNERS
AND LET THE LINE OF THOUGHT DIP DEEP INTO THE
STREAM."

— *Virginia Woolf*

Once you have started to dig deep into the myths, discarding those beliefs that don't connect to you, found a space, energized your creativity, and taken the path to nourish and transform, to grow into your true womanhood, then it's time to enter your secret chamber, your cocoon. Wrap yourself in love and luxury. Go so deep that you feel the sheer joy of connecting to your Divine Spirit. She has waited, and is she ready to laugh. The secret of life is not eternal youth. It's feeling so comfortable, so connected to your truth, your essence, that every day is sheer delight. No one can blow you over. No one can destroy you with a glance or word. Your Big Ass Hairtude is up, flying in the wind. You can laugh as loud as you want. Every day. You can belly dance, move your body, feel your soul. You are standing on the earth, and your fingers are touching clouds, your line of thought is deep in the stream.

The secret to connecting to your inner Divine, the real you, is to disconnect to all the parts of your life that have nothing to do with you. To climb into your cocoon, close the door. It is past time to shut the door on saying no to entering Your Personal Yes Room.

Your room is where you feel so good, being you, doing whatever you want—no matter what it is. There is no shame, pain, or guilt. In your cocoon is only you, celebrating your essence.

How does a Chic Cocoon make us feel?

Having our own space makes us feel safe. Human beings like being safe, and we feel a lot more comfortable daydreaming or getting into our own zone and exploring who we are when we are in a space that comforts us. This reminds me of being a kid holding onto my favorite little toy. It makes you feel like it's okay to be who you are because you're in your space. You're creating the cocoon that's wrapping you around and giving you permission to be who you are and allowing yourself to be vulnerable.

Want to know what kind of Cocoonista you are? Check out our website, CocoonChic.com, to find your style and tips to match.

We often think being vulnerable is a weakness, when actually, it is the first step to true strength. The more vulnerable you allow yourself to be, the stronger you become. When you release your secrets like butterflies, no one can reveal what is not hidden, you take back your power. You release your state of victimhood.

The Advantages of Quiet Time

Sometimes, it takes a bit of learning or unlearning to get to the idea that you have nothing to do but what you want to do. Boredom is the inspiration for creativity, as suggested by Peter Toohey in his book, *Boredom: A Lively History* http://yalepress.yale.edu/book.asp?isbn=9780300141108.

I know that boredom has fueled many of my projects, and apparently many famous creatives were compelled through boredom. I see kids inventing games all the time out of boredom. Embrace your boredom. Shut off the TV, the constant canned entertainment that demands only that you are a receiver. To be an effective participant in your life, not settling for other people's leftovers, you have to be in retreat with no distractions. You have to be your entertainer, an interesting lesson in getting to know yourself and to ask, "What do I do?" That is when it gets interesting because facing that boredom is when you realize that you do have deep desires and you need to harness it, plus get the benefit of enjoying the peace and quiet of escaping other people's demands. I think a huge part of what makes a woman feel so stressed is the voices, the clamor of need.

The most effective changes are when you can supply the missing ingredient. So if it's warmth that's missing, maybe you need to put in color. If there is no space to sit, or it doesn't feel cozy, maybe, create more dynamic furniture arrangements. If the walls feel blank, maybe think about bringing in and arranging art and accessories to please your eye. Do a favorite room check online or in a magazine, finding a room you adore and note what that room has that yours is missing. Or call in an expert.

7 Musts for your Cocoon:

- Comfy chair
- Good lighting
- Space to do whatever you want to do
- A view or inspiration
- Favorite piece
- Sounds you love
- Smells you adore

Personal Reflections for a Chic Cocoon

My Altar to Cocoonistadom. What would be the first piece?

Step one: To create a Chic Cocoon or the promise of a full-fledged one to come—a space. A Spiritual Retreat. A room would be ideal, but I would settle for a cozy corner or a window seat, a space for me to dream in, to grow in, to journal in.

And next would be the seat—The Royal Tush Holder.

When I think of that, **a fainting couch** comes to mind or a chair to curl up in. Perhaps it could be a **chaise** lounge, which is similar to the fainting couch. When I was growing up, my mom always had a chaise longue in her bedroom. That was the height of sophistication to me.

What would be your secret indulgence in your special spot or room?

Besides a **chaise** to linger on, one needs LIGHT. I am a huge fan of natural light. I always feel happier when in it. In my Chic Cocoon, I am planning a **skylight** above my chaise so I can dream in the sunlight and gaze at the stars at night. My Cocoon has French doors leading out to a glorious patio filled with potted plants and citrus trees – a walled garden of delights, including a table and chairs. There is nothing more cocoonalicious than eating outdoors on a good weather day.

This takes me back to my inner child. We had this wonderful house that was full of light and windows, with a huge veranda. There were many meals of happiness with heaped trays food.

Besides natural light, I believe a room to dream in needs a big ass chandelier to fit the style of said Diva. Mine will be playful as a jewel, befitting my Chic Retreat.

Ambient light to make the room glow requires concealed **up-lights** to circle the room. I can see floor lights in my dancing corner, a fireplace, candles, and dimmers for viewing the night sky, or to create a mood when friends are in.

Task lighting is essential for journaling, drawing, painting, and reading, so there will be light pooling down to work by, puck lights in the bookcases, spots on the art and in the trees, and the fountain. I love the idea of having a light control box, to take a nap in the day or to darken the room, so I can see the glimmer of the moon and stars from my comfy chair at night, while I sip a glass of Bordeaux and nibble on a tray of tasty treats.

What do you think about the importance of light, for your Chic Cocoon? What kind of mood and activities will you be indulging in?

Here is my personal list of what this Chic Cocoonista needs.

I envision natural light, windows, a chandelier, candles and candleholders, high ceilings, and a feeling of space to surround myself with.

Inspiration. A piece of art, a view, flowers or a handful of items collected with love.

A place to sit, a chaise, or a divinely comfortable chair with an ottoman.

A desk with a beautifully upholstered task chair on wheels for me to work in would be heavenly.

Scent, the smell of oranges, herbs, flowers. Color, the color of flowers, paint on the walls.

Texture: Luxurious textiles, so lots of lovely textiles, like a beautiful rug, rich curtains, with a soft drape, and a gorgeous throw that's all warm and cozy.

A cabinet to house notebooks, treasures, and inspiration.

A bookshelf for all my books; art, I love to surround myself with art and sculpture, photographs, and also Crayons, paint, paper, drawing utensils, and journals.

Sounds, like running water, bells, and music to dance to.

Create your list based on your desires and needs.

I think we women need to own our power. Stop giving it away and stop thinking of ourselves as a last resort. Create the room and sink into the sensuality of you. Refer Chapter 3 to find out what type of Chic Cocoon is for you.

Restraint

The larger picture in design is about how you use the space you claim.

Beware of cluttering up every surface with more stuff. This is not about buying stuff or moving every piece you love into your Chic Cocoon. It's about creating the space that makes you feel good, that suits your budget and personality. It's about creating a room that works for letting you relax and let go. You don't want to be lying in the room and thinking about how much dusting you have to do. Make the room shine for you and give it plenty of room for you to breathe.

Get creative with how you set up your room, or get help. First, figure out what you want and then check out online blogs, including mine, for how to make it happen.

My last home was a rental home. I warmed up the room with color and made it feel very comfortable and welcoming. I bought a rug in rich golds from a discount store and matched striped drapes. I pulled in pillows in a mix of reds and golds, and I painted the walls Soleil from Benjamin Moore, with Papaya trim. I put out my brass from my grandmother and some beaded baskets and candlesticks, many that I picked up at thrift stores. The big painting was a $20 find. I also created my own art and integrated it with my findings. The greatest complement people paid me when they came over was saying how they enjoyed being in my home, how comfortable it made them feel. "How did you make it work?" they would ask. By using things I found, hand-me-downs, or items I bought within my budget, I allowed myself to shine. I claimed my inner Diva in my own space. It was all about me. I love sitting in a room surrounded by personal pieces, mine or someone else's.

Even if it's a rental, you can still make your space work. If you can't paint the walls, you can change your room just by moving the furniture, bringing color in with accessories, tying it all together, and understanding that there's a flow of how it all goes together.

When you're shopping, don't buy everything you see, even if you love it—unless you need it and it works in your space. Make a list of what you need to buy and stick to it. Start from the ground up, unless you are just filling in. Carry samples of the colors you have in your room to guide your purchases.

The Power of Color

I organized a project with a woman from my local design group, to help a woman's shelter. Part of that project was adding color, with paint donated by Sherwin Williams. The other part involved all of us in our chapter collecting items and creating accessories we could use, for little or no cost. We had fabric donated, and some members sewed pillows and made quilts. One member collected frames from a consignment store, and we sprayed them all the same color. We filled the frames with art the residents made and some that we made ourselves with a little paper and paint. Some frames were left empty. It was pretty amazing. The most interesting part of it was that after the walls had been painted in warm inviting colors, the attitude of the residents changed. The colors in shades of warm greens and golds calmed the residents. When the first room was made over, it was hard to remember just how cold the room had been before. Color really does have restorative powers and can make you happy.

---

7 SIMPLE WAYS TO DECORATE
YOUR CHIC COCOON ON A BUDGET

1. If you have a chair that needs sprucing up, look for a cover up - buy a fitted cover, sew your own, or exchange services with a neighbor who does sew.

---

2. Need a piece of furniture and have limited resources? Look on places like Etsy.com for chairs. Check for sales at stores like Scandanavian Design, West Elm or Ballards, or a local consignment store. Think about using a garden chaise or chair that you can pretty up. Check with friends and family who have pieces they no longer need and troll garage sales. Small tables and bookshelves are easy to find. Paint or stain all the odd pieces in one or two colors.

3. Some fabulous lamps can be found at thrift stores. Spray your finding a bold new color and recover the shade, look for how-to's online. Check out big stores like Target or Ikea for simple fun options.

4. Keep your eye on sales. West Elm and Ballards also have great options in accessories.

5. Pillows are an easy way to brighten a drab chair. Check Etsy.com for some unusual options; Ikea has great covers and insets.

6. Check out online membership sites like Gilt.com, Joss & Main, and One Kings Lane for fabulous designer options on sale.

7. Rugs can make a room. Consider using a patchwork of smaller rugs (tape or have bound together). Check out online shopping sites or visit your local carpet store to have an offcut bound or find out when there are sales. Stores like Pottery Barn often have end of season sales. Macy's carries a wide range of rugs that are often on sale, too. Do some research and legwork.

> *"The thing women have yet to learn is nobody gives you power. You just take it."*
>
> ---ROSEANNE BARR

How does one claim their Chic Cocoon? Check out Chapter Three for places to grow in.

What do you mean by lifestyle?

We create a pattern of how we live daily, with small things. For example, every morning you make scones, and the whole family sits together to eat breakfast. Set up little habits to enhance your day, every day. Use the good china for the family. Sit in the garden for supper. Take a moment to bring in some flowers or leaf clippings from the garden and fill the sweet new vase you picked up at a garage sale. Start owning your lifestyle by creating the life you want to live. Decide how you want to feel by decorating your room to express you. You create that vision. If you can't afford an item you crave, create the look and make your own reality. Decorating is about mood and overall look—not so much about the actual individual items. So don't panic if what you have is less than your idea of perfect. I have worked in homes that have what appears to be nothing to work with. Without bringing in a single new thing, I have created a stylish haven for the owners.

Take our instant quiz to discover if you need to unlock your Chic Cocoon

- Are you feeling overwhelmed?

- Do you feel numb when you try to remember what you wanted in your life?

- Are you settling for survival?

- Are you staying in a safe relationship or job because of fear?

- When was the last time you took time for just you—more than two weeks ago?

- Is 90% of what you do because of obligation?

- Is guilt, shame, or fear your primary motivator?

If you answered yes to one of the above questions, you are in need of a serious pampering session. I suggest you run to your spare room and start clearing it out. Get ready to rediscover your inner woman and dance the Big Ass Hair Do Dance.

What type of Chic Cocoon are you?

Take our online quiz to find out what type of Chic Cocoon is your kind, along with tips to make it happen.
www.ChicCocoon.com

Seven Steps to Creating Your Selfish Space

The first is to declare your **intention.** You have to decide to do it. It's a big step. Conquer your fear and say, "Okay, I'm going to do this."

The second step is to **set your boundaries**. You have to decide. When are you going to do it? How are you going to make sure that you have that special time and space that other people can't intrude on? If you decide to use a room that's a shared room and you are taking over that room, you have to let the others know. Tell them they can no longer do their running or junking in this room because you have claimed it. Or explain when and what is out of bounds. Go so far as to get a lock and key that only you can open—a Big Ass Lock with an attitude. You schedule the time in your calendar and meet your appointment. That has to be sacred time and sacred space, so sacred in your mind that you don't give it up and people know about it.

Mark out your spot.

You've got to research and conquer. Get out of your head and search in your own home for the spot that you can use. Refer to Chapter 3 for seven possible spaces. Maybe you don't have a whole room, but perhaps there is a forgotten space, like a window seat. Find the place to use, and tell everybody about it. This space on the landing, this corner here in the bedroom, or this gazebo in the garden is mine. Don't mess with my space.

Arrive for the Appointment

"At this time, every day, I'm going to sit here for 30 minutes. Don't talk to me. Don't come and tell me anything unless there's a fire." You're not available to anyone. You're not going to come and fix anything. Somebody else will take care of it. You are not talking or listening.

> *"Women in particular need to keep an eye on their physical and mental health, because if we're scurrying to and from appointments and errands, we don't have a lot of time to take care of ourselves. We need to do a better job of putting ourselves higher on our own 'to do' list."*
>
> ---MICHELLE OBAMA

In the beginning, once you have claimed your spot and set the time, you can use the appointment to work on your space. While you are creating your space, your body and mind will be engaged in shifting. Pay attention to what comes up and journal about it.

Stand Strong.

In the actual space itself, empty out what's not inspiring and useful for your room. Pull out all the items that you hate, that are broken, had nowhere to go, and sentimental items that you don't need or want. What do you do with the stuff you hate? If you hate it, let it go. Unless you desperately need that object, then you can paint it, cover it up, or decorate it. Let go of all the things you no longer need. If they're heirlooms, give them to a family member or sell them. Get them out of your life because you need to open up the space for new things.

Don't hesitate or ponder. Just ask yourself, "Do I need this item?" If yes, put it where it goes. If no, throw it out (or toss it on the giveaway pile). Space is more important than any item you think you might need. Your life, your value, is greater than any item. No guilty consciences are allowed. Did somebody you love or admire give you this? SO WHAT? Each of us has only a little space we can call our own in this life. Don't let guilt or good behavior dictate what goes into your space. Your instincts, your real inner woman is in charge. Do the happy dance, and toss the uglies out of your life.

YOUR COCOON ON THE GO

Cocoon to go: Keep a packed bag with essential Cocoonista materials—a pen, a journal, a candle, an inspiring book, a picture of a painting or nature that inspires you, and your favorite sachet. When you travel, if you commute—your cocoon in a bag will always be ready—just because you won't be in your room doesn't mean you can't be ready to cocoon at a moment's notice.

How Do You Get Your Chic Cocoon Mojo On?

7 Steps to Creating Chic Cocoon Bliss:

1. Examine your space: What do you like about it, what do you dislike? What can you change? Let it all sink in.

2. Make a plan: List the steps of action that you need to take to move your space from dumpy to divine.

3. Dump or hide the clutter: Cover up the open shelf with a curtain, or organize your files and brick-a-brac in fun boxes.

4. Placement: Face your desk or chaise in the optimum position – where you will have the best view.

5. Create it: Make a wall of inspiration – your accolades, guides, mentors, beloved family members and friends, and memories that ignite you.

6. Light it up: Bring in a Big Ass Jewel of a light, add candles on a tray or in holders.

7. Package: Pull in awesome artwork or a fabulous rug and connect the space with color and emotion that speaks to you.

Pulling Your Feel Good Space Together

We're talking about revitalizing, re-energizing, changing space, and looking at it differently. We're grouping things.

On the Wall

Do group art. It makes a statement.

Don't put individual pictures all over every wall; it just scatters people's attention. There's nowhere to focus. Your eye reads this as distracting. You need focus in a room, just like you do in a piece of art, with spaces for your eyes to rest. Groupings are very powerful. Test your grouping by laying out the artwork in the design in which you want to hang it. You could also cut out templates sized to replicate the art and play around with it on the wall. Pair up sets of pictures and add in pairs of small shelves or dramatic lights. Use multiples of an item in different sizes, like ceiling medallions or another collection you have lying around. Your guitars can be art, so can your collection of angels. Even magazine tear outs can be framed in a grouping. Put a branch across a wall and hang hearts on ribbons from it, or little birds. There is no end to what can become wall art. Group your ornaments for impact. Use pairs and odd numbers. Go for a bold look by using a few large items, instead of lots of little items. Don't rush to fill up the space. Keep it clean and simple and uncluttered. You don't want to be surrounded by distractions.

Create Your Chic Cocoon in One Day or Less

Note: Moving furniture can cause injury or pain. Invest in tools to make it easier. Furniture slides are a terrific help when moving big items. Be sensible and don't overdo it. Get help and take precautions. Check out other tools for moving furniture at your local hardware store.

Have a hammer, a drill, and the right nails handy for hanging large or awkward items. Be prepared before you rush in.

You Have Your Room

1. Empty it out, completely. If you have something that's broken and you're not going to fix it, get rid of it. If you have something you like but you hate the color, think about how you can change it. Sometimes by altering a piece with paint or another application, you create a new life for it.

2. Ask yourself what you are going to be doing in this room. What features can you emphasize, and what do you want to minimize? Where do you want to sit? What is the best view? Where does the light fall? Will you be watching TV in your room? Do you want to look outside? Is there a door to go outside? Do you have a fireplace? Understand the function of your space. Understand what you need to put in it. Look around the house, the garage, a thrift store, or turn to a friend or neighbor who has things they are no longer using to unleash possibilities.

3. Making the first move. Place the biggest item in the room first, facing the most interesting view, the focal point. Put in your chair or chaise to face the view. This is about what you want. If you have a lovely window, then face your chair to the window, if that feels good to you. If you are putting in a bed and you are not going to use it much, give your chair pride of placement. If you are bringing in a desk to work at, which you will be using a lot, place that in the optimum space, with the chair facing the view. You might want to put the desk at an angle or put it against the wall, depending on how big it is. Perhaps you want to place the desk facing the window and put the chair behind it. Maybe you want to put in a cabinet or a bookshelf to fill with books and treasures. Make sure you have enough room to walk around and feel comfortable

in the room. You don't want to fill up all the space. The key to a room that feels luxurious is to keep it simple and open. A feeling of space helps your creativity.

Perhaps you have a chair and a chaise, or a bar, an armoire, an ottoman, or a coffee table—all these items take up volume and need to be placed with care. Since this is a one-day activity, feel free to use an item as a placeholder—for example, a garden chair. You can replace it with what you really want when the opportunity arises. By placing all the pieces you need right away, you put your room to use, and you have an idea of what will really work instead of your placeholder.

4. Once the big items are placed, you want to add in your rug, if you have one. A rug can really bring a space together, especially when you have different pieces you are trying to meld. Place the rug under the chair legs or close to the furniture. A rug also grounds a room. You need to have a rug that is big enough to make a statement. A 3 x 5 rug would typically be too small, but sometimes you don't have a choice. You can use the rug you have, or look around in any room to see what's available. If you are planning on getting a new rug, pick a color and design that relates to the furniture in your room. Sometimes you can pull in two rugs. If you are creating two spaces—one to sit at and one to write in—and your room is large, you can use a rug to delineate each space. Think of a rug like a piece of art.

5. Place your side table next to your chair so you can reach over with ease for your journal or magazines. Are there other pieces of small furniture to place? Do you have an ottoman or a chest?

6. Place your lamp behind your chair so that you have good lighting when you need it. Make sure you have enough light for whatever you need to do. Put a lamp on your desk.

7. Once the furniture is placed, start figuring out where you will place your art.

Don't place pictures too high; consider optimal viewing height for when you're in the room. If you are looking at a favorite piece from your chair, hang it so you have the best view when you are sitting down. If you have lots of artwork or small pictures, group them on the wall together. If you don't have any art, create your own or use some of your kids' drawings. You can also pick up a picture book at the thrift store and frame the pages you like.

Finally, find that perfect piece that will glow in your Cocoon.

Gather the inspirational items that will honor you in your space. If you see something that you love from another room, bring it in to your space, like a favorite throw to give you that little bit of joy in your new sanctuary. Go through your home and find some things that have meaning to you and put them in your space. It may be a piece of art or a photograph that you love, bring it in and see if it works, if you have a spot to place it.

The idea is to use only what you need and to be very selective about what you pick and where you place it. The art and accessories you select should give you pleasure. This doesn't require expensive items. Be creative in pulling together found objects, thrift store discoveries, and admired pieces from family members. Check out my website and other online sources for ideas on how to organize and display treasures. Bring in all those pieces that you love and start placing them. This could include a collection of something that you can display in your room. Don't overcrowd the surfaces. You need space, room to breathe, and a place to create. The rule of thumb is to use odd numbers in a grouping. You can use books to add height. Put a bowl of flowers on top of a book or mix up books, photographs, and collectables on shelves.

Leave room on the table for your glass or journal. If you don't have many accessories, think outside the box. Use a tray of candles, a box of marbles, or a potted plant. Bring in your boom box or your musical instrument, if that is important to you. Maybe you want a fountain—if so, find the place that works best. Try to group all the small things together in one or two places so that a clump of items visually becomes one. Keep the groupings simple. Typically, we cannot display everything that we love in one room. Again, you want your space to feel free and open. Add a couple of fun pillows and a basket for magazines, maybe some big plants to soften the room. Flowers and candles add color. Bring your personality in and whatever else you need to connect to your inner Spirit. Treat yourself to an amazing journal; include a couple of terrific pens and place it in your little space, your fire starter.

8. Window treatments depend on the window and whether you need privacy or not. You may decide to use what is there, or drape a piece of fabric from the rod, or change the blinds. Hang a sun catcher or two in the window for fun. The window treatments can be tweaked once you pull the space together with your colors and the textures of your pillows and rugs. Take time to decide what will work. Check out catalogues and online window covering stores for inspiration.

For more details and ideas, check out my website www.chiccocoon.com.

If you are creating a room that serves a dual purpose, like a guest room or your office/ meditation space, the process is the same.

However, you will have more pieces to work with.

You can have a bed, like a divan with pillows and a fabulous throw, on one side so you can lie in it and read magazines or journal. Remember, the primary purpose of the room is for you, so put the focus on creating your haven. The other function of the room is less important, so it is okay for it to be hidden.

What if I don't have money to buy anything new right now? Can I make my space work?

Yes, if you follow steps 1 through 7 of a one-day makeover above, you don't need to buy anything. You don't need to do it all in one day, either. We often have plenty of things, like a garden or rocking chair, or folding chairs can work, as well as little tables. You can find some really cool stuff from garage sales and thrifts. They often have amazing stuff, little tables, fabulous jugs and bowls, and terrific art. Make a list of what your essentials are. Find your little treasures and then pull them together. Let's say you find a chair from somewhere in the house and you put it in your place—now look for a rug, if you have one. If you don't have one, then maybe you can do without a rug for a while. And then you can add a lamp from somewhere in your house—if you don't have one, you can find one fairly inexpensively at Goodwill or at a garage sale, usually for a couple of dollars. Maybe you have a friend who's getting rid of a lamp. If you walk around your house with your list of items, you will find things for your room. It's very possible to pull it all from your space. Don't worry about taking something from somewhere else, unless that is an essential item in that space. If you see a painting that you absolutely love, bring it into your space. Pull your Chic Cocoon together. See the seed of your room taking shape. Even with just a floor, a pillow, and a piece of art or a plant, you room is born.

SELFISH ACTION

Go to the spa and treat yourself to a facial or a manicure and pedicure, and visualize yourself sinking into your delicious Chic Cocoon, bathed in light. Are you dreaming of a window with a view? If your room has no view, make one. Visit some online art stores and find a wall-sized poster that will bring out the Cocoonista in you.

Have a window, but no view? Hang some pretty sheers to let the light in, or cover the window with film that is translucent. Check out your local big box store for many choices in film. If you can't put in a skylight, maybe a sun tunnel will be a happy addition.

What about a big, bold, sassy light to read by at night? Take a walk through a lighting store and pay attention to the ones that turn you on. There is nothing quite like a bit of drama that comes with a Big Ass Light. Dark corners can easily be lit with up-lights, and they are very affordable. Thrift stores are wonderful places to score lights with attitude. Remember you can change the shade and color of the lamp. There are lots of custom choices where you can choose your lamp shape, color, and shade that are available for a higher price. You can cover an old lampshade in a fun fabric and add a little fringing, too. Candles are so tantalizing; they come in such lovely scents and colors. Group a bunch on an old tray. Light feels good, so be sure you have enough for your needs.

Visit some online light stores or hit the local big box stores or antique shops to get your dreaming juice flowing.

CHAPTER SEVEN

Soar to Roar

"AS A WOMAN, I HAVE NO COUNTRY. AS A WOMAN, I WANT NO
COUNTRY. AS A WOMAN, MY COUNTRY IS THE WHOLE WORLD."
— *Virginia Woolf*

Cocooning is an attitude. Once you get in the habit, you will
be able to summon your Inner Divine at a moment's notice.

Discover and explore your own Nirvana, your personal
spiritual retreat, and find the joy to soar at will.

Live by your rules, in your Chic Cocoon. Whether you
crave certainty, variety, love or recognition, you can begin
putting the habits in place that will serve you and place you
squarely at the feast of life.

I know that what a woman needs is a room of her own,
the silence to listen to no voice but hers. Whether your space
is imaginary, still in the dream stage, or if you have a room
that will fit a hundred small rooms within it, you are taking a
huge step for earthkind. Your act of selfishness is one that
will reward us all. The reverberation of women touching
Nirvana, of reaching the roof garden, and bursting the glass
ceiling will be so huge we might very well get to see millions
of butterflies in flight.

I believe that life is hopeful. I also know that women are
the most powerful beings on earth. We have all the tools to
change the world, one room at a time. You may not have a
grand scheme for your life, and that is perfect. You are
perfect. Take advantage of the domino effect, one tiny move
strikes another and castles tumble. I challenge you to do your
part to cut a hole in the wall and bring in some light. Allow

yourself that view to breathe, and when your lungs expand and you breathe out, send forth a tiny butterfly on wings of joy.

I am so happy that we are not weighed down by as many myths as Virginia Woolf and the women of her generation. I am also grateful that they lit the way for us.

I have thought long and hard about a woman's voice and a woman's choice.

Women need to invest in their Big Ass Hair Do and claim their spot in the line. Yes, reality bites, myths live on, and some people can't let go of what they learned. Men and women still bitch about big hair and assorted body parts.

The myth exists and so does big hair. I say we lean into the wind and let the hair fly. Embrace our secret selves, big hair and all, and know that just like Samson, we need that hair. Curly and wild or straight and narrow, no matter how your hair curls or how your butt wiggles, flaunt it. Take no notice of people that tell you that your hair is too big or your butt is too wild. We need to embrace our big ass selves with our big do attitude.

As long as we buy into the myth and fall for the diversion that women must not stand out for the wrong reasons, we will continue to be distracted from our goals.

What is our recourse? We need a surprise attack—the bold move. Let the real inner woman stroll to the Queen's table and dig in. Totally ignore the naysayers. We can flip our Big Ass Hair Do Attitude and keep on walking, with our eye on the prize.

Let us show our tough inner core, the one that is focused and fabulous.

So men or women may whistle myth, but we will be both focused on our goals and laughing to see them use that old trick again. Be proud of your Big Ass Hair. Love it.

Embrace your ultimate womanhood and every part that makes you an individual—your hair and your attitude. Remember, it's a game that we aim to win. Keep laughing, shaking your hair and keep moving on. There is no shame in flaunting who you are. Leave guilt, shame, and apology outside, where it belongs. They are just baggage you no longer need or require.

Merge your masculine and feminine sides and dive into the battle and romance of leading your life as a winner.

In closing, I want to say that life is about the laughter. The more you cleave to happiness, to bringing joy on the journey, the greater the experience.

A lot of what is missing in our worlds and why we need these rooms is precisely because we have banished our feminine and, yes, even our masculine, within to blend into the landscape. It is time to laugh loudly with our inner Divine. Bring her to the table. I promise your life will be a most delicious, rewarding banquet.

To the Big Ass Hair Do Attitude and your own personal Chic Cocoon!

I encourage you to get started right away. Drop me a line on my website www.chiccococoon.com

I am looking forward to hearing the tale of your room.

My mom made this saying up years ago, and I am sharing it with you to live by:

"Don't look down to your feet when you can look up to the stars."

SELFISH ACTION

Bring your sexy, sassy, fabulous body and mind combo, your Big Ass Hair Do out of hiding. Do the most outrageous thing on your list. No one can resist a confident woman. Take up a pole dancing class or dive into learning salsa. If you have dreamed of parachuting or air ballooning, set a date and do it for you.

Joy Rising

Feel gladness in your heart for what is in your life. The more you focus on something, the more you bring it around you.

People talk about not sweating the small stuff. I say find joy in the small stuff. Each day should be a blessing, full of sweet moments that create your lifestyle.

Trust in you and your abundance. Practice daily rituals to connect with your inner Divine.

Increase your own happiness factor by cherishing you, for 10 to 60 minutes a day.

Take time to be a Cocoonista. Wrap yourself up by practicing safe Selfishness.

Add in a splash of gratitude and joy for all the small things in your life that make it sweet.

Float up to meet joy.

The Happiness Factor

World peace begins with your inner peace.

Give only as much as you can and give to yourself first.

Don't hold onto things you no longer need.

Do what you love.

Hire out the rest.

Dance daily.

See abundance everywhere.

Give with complete joy.

Accept help willingly.

Know people want to help you.

Everyone does the best they can.

Live each moment in the moment.

Kick the myths to the curb.

Let go of anything or anyone who doesn't get it.

Be confident in moving into your Big Ass Hair Do Attitude.

Celebrate you daily.

"When you master serving yourself, you have the capacity to serve others generously and without resentment. The self-actualized woman is healthy, abundant and at peace. Only in taking care of ourselves can we be around long enough to see future generations thrive. There is nothing heroic in being a selfless martyr. In fact, I daresay if women were

self-ish' enough to put their Life Purposes first, the need for charity would be eradicated in our lifetimes. Let's hold THAT vision."

--- BAETH DAVIS,
YOUR PROSPERITY PURPOSE MENTOR
WWW.YOURPURPOSE.COM

ACKNOWLEDGEMENTS

Thank you to my family, my dearest mother, my darling daughter, and my incredible sister. A special thanks to Darcie Newton, Franziska San Pedro, Fiona Stoltze, and Louise Eddington for being the first Cocoonistas.

Thank you to Barbara Barry for her inspiration and incredible kindness.

My deepest admiration for all the women who served others before themselves, I am hoping this book will guide you to becoming a Cocoonista.

A special thanks to Virginia Woolf, without whom there would be no room of my own.

Appreciation for friends and mentors, including Heidi Sloss, for all her support. Alicia Dunams, if you had not been there, this book would not have been written. Ann Evanston, Ana Maria Sanchez, Pamela Landers, Lynn V. Hawkins, Phyllis Garland, Brandy Mychals, Ava Johnson, Sandy Dixon, Kimberly Des Jardins, Adryenn Ashley, Maria Killam, Patti McKenna for all her terrific help on the book and patience with my changes, Zoe Lonergan for the beautiful cover, Rie Langdon for wonderful insight, Alara Castell, Maridel Bowes, Shelley Holmes, Tambra Harck, Lauren Shelby, Corinne Friedman, Jessica Ryan, Philip Bewley, Catherine Grasky, Keri Ofshe, Corinne Pluska, Judy Peebles, Rita Brennan Freay, Donna McCord, Jillian Todd, Yvonne Hall, Corinna Mori for her beautiful garden setting, Eedit Bareket for her assistance and insightful feedback, and all of my dear friends too numerous to name and appreciated gratefully, colleagues and assistants who inspired me, believed in me, and encouraged me. Goldie, my soul dog, you made it all worthwhile.

Jennifer Duchene is a product of her own life experiences. Growing up in South Africa in a home where entertaining was an everyday occurrence, style was absorbed, observed, and adored.

Jennifer completed the FIDER accredited Interior and Environmental Design Program at UCLA.

After several life and job changes, including mothering her daughter, and many moves, Duchene studied Redesign and started her own business, focusing on helping her clients create delicious spaces with what they already owned—spaces that allow women to love themselves, combining design aesthetics and the essence of the woman inside the room.

Clients have called Duchene an excellent listener, highly creative with the ability to mix odd elements and to be flexible in guiding them to a fuller, richer space to live in, while honoring their collections and tastes.

Jennifer is a lifelong learner, with a love of sharing knowledge in a witty, ebullient way. To her, everything is fascinating. Duchene has come to realize the importance of pulling together her talents to create spaces that honor women, giving them room not only to breathe, but to fly.

Wikipedia Virginia Woolf Wikipedia
http://en.wikipedia.org/wiki/Virginia_Woolf

The Virginia Woolf Society
http://www.virginiawoolfsociety.co.uk
The International Virginia Woolf Society
http://www.utoronto.ca
Available Virginia Woolf texts http://www.penguin.com

A Room of One's Own by Virginia Woolf
http://www.library.csi.cuny.edu/dept/history/lavender/own
room
http://www.amazon.com/Room-Ones-Own-Virginia-
Woolf/dp/0156787334

Virginia Woolf Quotes

"A woman must have money and a room of her own if she is to write fiction." — Virginia Woolf (*A Room of One's Own*)

"One cannot think well, love well, sleep well, if one has not dined well." (P. 18) — Virginia Woolf (*A Room of One's Own*)

"Lock up your libraries if you like, but there is no gate, no lock, no bolt that you can set upon the freedom of my mind." — Virginia Woolf (*A Room of One's Own*)

"Literature is strewn with the wreckage of men who have minded beyond reason the opinions of others." –Virginia Woolf (*A Room of One's Own*)

"By hook or by crook, I hope that you will possess yourselves of money enough to travel and to idle, to contemplate the future or the past of the world, to dream over books and loiter at street corners and let the line of thought dip deep into the stream." –Virginia Woolf (*A Room of One's Own*)

"No need to hurry. No need to sparkle. No need to be anybody but oneself." — Virginia Woolf (*A Room of One's Own*, and *Three Guineas*)
Three Guineas by Virginia Woolf
http://www.goodreads.com/book/show/18854.Three_Guineas

"As a woman, I have no country. As a woman, I want no country. As a woman, my country is the whole world." – Virginia Woolf (*Three Guineas*, 1938, ch. 3)

"It is in our idleness, in our dreams, that the submerged truth sometimes makes its way to the surface." — Virginia Woolf

Other Quotes and References

Marya Mannes
http://en.wikipedia.org/wiki/Marya_Mannes
http://www.quotationspage.com/quotes/Marya_Mannes

You Can Heal Your Life by Louise Hay
http://www.louisehay.com

Harry Frederick Harlow
http://en.wikipedia.org/wiki/Harry_Harlow
http://clearwater-uk.com/MyBlog/2010/02/28/five-monkeys-a-banana-and-corporate-culture

Nava Atlas http://navaatlasart.com
http://www.craftingfiction.com/2011/03/self-acceptance-a-hard-fought-battle-even-for-accomplished-authors

Baeth Davis, Your Purpose Prosperity Mentor
http://YourPurpose.com

Andrea Dworkin
http://thinkexist.com/quotation/women_have_been_taught
_that-for_us-
the_earth_is/256651http://www.nostatusquo.com/ACLU/d
workin

Lucille Ball
http://en.wikipedia.org/wiki/Lucille_Ball
http://www.goodreads.com/author/quotes/86608.Lucille_B
all

Mark Vernon, Author and Philosopher
http://www.markvernon.com
http://www.markvernon.com/friendshiponline/dotclear

Claim your free 7 Selfish Sex Tips report
www.chiccocoon.com/selfishspacessextips
http://www.ruemag.com/ http://dabblemag.com

Marcia Cooner, *Learn More Now*, Chapter 10 "Optimize Your
Environment"
http://marciaconner.com/learnmorenow/index.html

Corinne Friedman, www.artfulshoes.com

W. Clement Stone,
http://en.wikipedia.org/wiki/W._Clement_Stone

Tina Seelig, Executive Director for the Stanford Technology
Ventures Program (STVP), the entrepreneurship center at
Stanford University's School of Engineering—author of *What
I Wish I Knew When I Was Twenty: On Making Your Place in the
World*

http://havefundogood.blogspot.com/2011/02/tina-seeligs-9-ways-to-unlock-your.html
http://soe.stanford.edu/research/layoutMSnE.php?sunetid=tseelig
Psychologist Dr. Mary W. Meagher's Texas A&M University Study, http://www.fi.edu/learn/brain/stress.html

Oprah Winfrey, O Magazine http://www.oprah.com/own

Elizabeth Donati, *The Ultimate Allowance*
http://ultimateallowancebook.com/blog/?p=20

Definition of OPINION
http://www.merriam-webster.com/dictionary/opinion

Susan Ariel Rainbow Kennedy (Succulent Wild Woman)
http://www.planetsark.com

Mary Catherine Bateson, Writer and cultural anthropologist
www.marycatherinebateson.com

Peter Toohey in his book, *Boredom: A Lively History*
http://yalepress.yale.edu/book.asp?isbn=9780300141108

Benjamin Moore Paint
Soleil AF-330 http://www.benjaminmoore.com/en-us/paint-color/soleil
Papaya 957 http://www.benjaminmoore.com/en-us/paint-color/papaya

Roseanne Barr
http://www.biography.com/womens-history/quotes.jsp
http://www.roseanneworld.com/blog/home.php

Michelle Obama
http://www.listentohappiness.com/articles/encouraging-quotes-from-michelle-obama/
http://en.wikipedia.org/wiki/Michelle_Obama

Resources

Mind Mapping
http://www.mindtools.com/pages/article/newISS_01.htm

www.ChicCocoon.com
www.JenniferDuchene.com

Online Magazines

Sartorialist http://www.thesartorialist.blogspot.com

Rue Magazine http://www.ruemag.com

Dabble Magazine http://dabblemag.com

Stores: online and brick and mortar

Home Depot www.homedepot.com

Target www.target.com

Lowes Home Improvement www.lowes.com

TJ Max www.tjmaxxhomegoods.com

Pottery Barn www.potterybarn.com

Horchow www.horchow.com

Ballards www.ballarddesigns.com

Ikea www.ikea.com

Restoration Hardware. www.restorationhardware.com

Scandanavian Designs www.scandinaviandesigns.com

West Elm http://www.westelm.com

Gilt.com http://www.gilt.com

One Kings Lane https://www.onekingslane.com

Joss & Main http://www.jossandmain.com

Etsy, Etsy.com

The Hive http://creatingthehive.com

Thrift Stores

Goodwill www.goodwill.org

St Vincent de Paul http://www.svdpusa.org/salv

Salvation Army www.salvationarmyusa.org

Fabulous People (who have been very kind to me)

Sandy Dixon
The Staging Trainer www.TheStagingTrainer.com
Certification Training Programs, Marketing Products and Coaching

Darcie Newton Discovering Delicious
Devoted to finding all things Delicious
http://www.discoveringdelicious.com

Louise Edington
Fabulous and Fearless
http://louiseedington.com

Fiona Stotlze
Inspired Art and Living
http://fionastolze.com

Franziska San Pedro
Abstract Impressionism.
http://franziskasanpedro.com
http://www.flavordesigns.com

Jillian Todd
Portrai Couture
http://www.jilliantodd.com

Maridel Bowes
"Shaking up a cocktail of spirit and soul with a twist of laughter"
http://www.evolvingjourney.com

Brandy Mychals
Creator of the Character Code System™
BrandyMychals.com

Alara Castell
Your Sassy Spiritual Guide
www.alaracastell.com

Ann Evanston MA
 Motivational speaker, coach and consultant
 annevanston.com
Capture the Warrior Within
www.WarriorPreneur.com

Judy Peebles
Experience the positive power of the pen!
The Journaling Jenius™
www.TheJournalingJenius.com

Judy Stone-Goldman
The Reflective Writer
www.thereflectivewriter.com

Sharon Jakubecky
Certified Alexander Technique Teacher, Poise Performance Coach, and Choreographer
 www.AlexanderTechniqueLA.com
 www.SharonJakubecy.com

Shivie Cook
The Cook and Butler. Living life on purpose
TheCookandButler.com
Tambra Harck
Spiritual Mentor, Author,Speaker
Web: TambraHarck.com
Book: SacredTruthsBook.com

Kelly Galea - The Design Biz Coach
http://thedesignbizcoach.com

Jessica Gordon Ryan
Memoirist, Social Media Expert, Writer, Editorial and
Creative Director of Lifestyle blogs... by day - Champagne
and Gimlet Drinker by night!
The Entertaining House

Shelley Holmes
Researcher/analyst for @TheDailyBasics
http://thedailybasics.com

Lauren   Shelby,   Interior   Designer   Spaces   Within.
http://spaceswithin.com

Barbara Barry
Barbara Barry, Inc.
www.barbarabarry.com

CPSIA information can be obtained at www.ICGtesting.com
Printed in the USA
BVOW010000131011

273506BV00004B/1/P